Railways and War
since 1917

The author and illustrator would like to thank all those who have helped them in the preparation of this book, in particular the Royal Corps of Transport at Longmoor and the Imperial War Museum.

RAILWAYS AND WAR since 1917

by
DENIS BISHOP

and
W. J. K. DAVIES

LONDON
BLANDFORD PRESS

First published in 1974
by Blandford Press Ltd
167 High Holborn, London WC1V 6PH

© Blandford Press 1974

ISBN 0 7137 0706 2

All rights reserved. No part of this book may be reproduced or transmitted in any form or by any means, electronic or mechanical, including photocopying, recording or by any information storage and retrieval system, without permission in writing from the publisher.

Colour section printed by Colour Reproductions Ltd, Billericay
Text printed in Great Britain by
Richard Clay (The Chaucer Press) Ltd, Bungay, Suffolk

INTRODUCTION

The previous volume in this series ostensibly took the story up to 1918. This one slips back a little because there were many aspects of World War 1 we were not able to encompass in the space available. Notable among these were the long drawn-out struggle between Austrians and Italians in appallingly difficult mountain country; the German standard war locomotives and what happened to them; and certain events on the Western Front. Perhaps the most interesting of these was the Austro-Italian campaign fought out along the Dolomite Alps under conditions in which mule-paths were often the only available transport routes. As a result, the Austrians in particular constructed some extremely lengthy narrow-gauge railways up the craggy valleys, supplementing them with some of the first really practicable ropeway systems. Indeed it is not too much to claim that the present-day cable cars so common in tourist resorts would have taken far longer to develop without the lessons learnt in this campaign.

In Salonika, too, the French and British started with horse-drawn 'tramways' but built up a series of quite lengthy locomotive-hauled 60cm gauge railways to supply their static fronts on the Struma and Dvina. Otherwise it was mainly a case of tearing railways up: in Palestine the legendary Lawrence methodically blew up the various sections of the newish Hedjaz railway as soon as they were completed or repaired. Odd trains and stations in various stages of disrepair litter the southern deserts to this day. In South-West Africa it was the Germans who ripped up their own railway line behind them as they retreated inland, hiding the vital parts to the annoyance of pursuing South African forces. Even on the French front there are minor epics which escaped chronicling—the way for instance in which the western 'bit' of the massive Belgian secondary system turned itself into a military tramway; the considerable part played in the supply of Verdun by an inconsiderable metre-gauge company: it was completely overshadowed by the notorious 'Voie Sacrée' road link but nevertheless provided about a third of the garrison's supplies.

And after the war came the reckoning. Railways, although badly knocked about themselves, played a major role in repairing the damage caused by four years of devastation. Enemy locomotives and stock prized because of their efficiency were 'requisitioned' as reparations for almost every European country and they lasted a long time: there were survivors working until the mid-1960s in some places. Even Portugal, which had a different gauge to the rest, had a number of machines specially built as acknowledgement of her help on the Western Front. More immediately, the existing light railway systems also played a great part in rehabilitating the areas through which they ran. In France considerable mileages were used for some years east of Arras as passenger-carrying lines and even when restoration was complete many stayed on in seasonal use as agricultural lines. They were ideal for transporting that dull but essential vegetable the sugar-beet which has to be harvested in great quantities during a very concentrated period of the year. The 60cm lines were simple; they ran right across country, and were already there complete with fully depreciated locomotives and stock! Once again they survived right into the 1960s and, as one might expect, some of the last survivors were run by those efficient German 0-8-0Ts. (These, just to clear up an incidental point, were officially not 'feldbahn lokomotiven' but 'brigade-lokomotiven'; they were intended for use by the formed railway brigades attached to armies.) In Salonika and Mesopotamia the lines were removed as soon as clearing up had finished; in South-West Africa they were partially regauged and restored; in Italy most of the better engineered ones were retained and turned into proper secondary railways.

World War 1 was the war to end wars . . . but that did not prevent the military from keeping a very lively interest in railways in all their forms. In France the 60cm gauge artillery railways continued to trundle around their massive fortifications. In England the large bases built up at some cost were retained, Longmoor in particular becoming a focus for experimentation and training. In Germany it was no doubt sensible that immediate postwar construction was of the former standard Prussian types. It was more ominous that the new standard locomotives (Einheitsloks) introduced from 1925 on were still designed with an eye to passing other people's loading gauges. Yet the main connection of railways with war purposes was in the expanding colonies, especially of France and Italy. The railways of French Morocco had for some time been run by the military, and from 1935 the Italians in Eritrea and Somaliland developed the railways with the dual role of supplying their military conquests and then acting as lifelines for the resulting colonial administrations. Of the major powers in Europe perhaps only the Germans were still thinking really seriously of using railways extensively for purely military purposes. England and France were prepared to organise their civilian systems in an emergency to handle mass movements—supply and evacuation—but they were not intending to attack anyone. Germany was intending to and her production facilities were not nearly sufficient to provide and maintain a fully motorised army. Hence not only supplies but the bulk of her line infantry divisions would have to be moved to the battle zones by railway—and a feature of the German plans for 'lightning war' was that the battle zones would advance rapidly. Indeed the plans depended on the military breakthrough being so swift that rail facilities would remain largely undamaged, and so it proved in 1940. Once again a very efficient military railway department appeared to triumph over all obstacles and even, when the Russian campaign opened in 1941, proved capable of regauging hundreds of miles of the Russian 5ft 6in. gauge. Nor surprisingly, the two major German freight locomotive designs, the light 2-10-0s of class 50 and the heavy ones of class 44 proved rapidly adaptable into the simplified Kriegsloks-war locomotives—of classes 52 and 42. Tens of thousands were produced during the war, although there were never enough to keep pace with the destruction caused by Allied forces.

As soon as the war got fully into its stride, first the British and then, when they came in, the Americans also produced standard 2-8-0 and 2-10-0 freight locomotives. The American ones were a special design. The British, as in World War 1, adapted an existing design in the shape of Sir William Stanier's heavy goods 2-8-0 of the L.M.S. Both also produced six-coupled shunting tank locomotives and, a new feature, standard diesels. The American major design was B-B diesel electric, the British one an 0-6-0DE. The Germans had a standard 0-6-0D too but it was diesel hydraulic. World War 2 proved even more of a strain on railways than the previous one had done. The civilian systems came under particular pressure owing to the threefold handicaps of vastly increased traffic, increasing shortage of manpower, and damage from aerial attack. In World War 1 railways were the safest form of transport. Between 1939 and 1945 they were often one of the most dangerous for their very advantages of providing bulk transport made them desirable targets. Their tracks, yards, stations and bridges were very vulnerable to bombing and the science of aerial warfare had advanced rapidly during the intervening years of peace. Besides bombs, aircraft cannon had developed too; a steam locomotive with its boiler and firebox riddled from cannon shell was just as much *hors de combat* as one with its wheels blown off by a shell and both sides took full advantage of the havoc aircraft could wreak.

Railways also had one further handicap. Their well-equipped workshops were excellent for producing all manner of war materials—a works that could build hundred-ton locomotives had little difficulty in producing the heavy armour components for thirty-ton tanks. In consequence, while they helped the war effort in this way, their own maintenance and repairs suffered and grimy trains leaking steam from various pores became a common sight in Britain and in the occupied countries where many facilities had been appropriated by the occupiers. The Germans themselves were more realistic and at least until 1944 they gave a high priority to railway maintenance and repair. They were also adept at repairing damage and at making it appear much greater than it was so that rail services were not disrupted so much as our propaganda made out. A classic example was the case of the important Bielefeld viaduct which, in the manner of bridges, withstood near misses for several years. By the time a bomb had been developed which could undermine it the Reichsbahn had prudently built a double-track diversion down into the valley and up the other side. Well camouflaged, this enabled traffic to continue flowing steadily over a route that by allied calculations should have been entirely out of action.

Destruction did not only interfere with main-line railway services to the war effort, however. In Europe it also sometimes affected the services to the local communities who were now mainly dependent on their local—often narrow-gauge—tramway or light railway. More than once R.A.F. pilots returning from a sortie lightheartedly reported that they had 'strafed an Emmett' without realising that the little train left wreathed in steam and with wounded passengers was not helping the enemy at all. Indeed the 'small railways' of Europe were doing their best to keep communities in the occupied areas alive and supplied. With the main lines sequestered and petrol almost non-existent they were often the only way. The Belgian S.N.C.V. (secondary railways) system even ran long regular coal trains from the industrial areas into the big cities over its connected systems of metre-gauge track.

Less extensive systems in France and Holland regained their original role of taking produce to and from market and even, on the zonal border between occupied and unoccupied France in particular, indulged in the odd spot of smuggling. They were always subject to day-to-day hazards and they had their poignant moments such as the last train from Oradour-S-Glâne which by some whim was allowed to clear that unfortunate village before its inhabitants were ruthlessly massacred by the S.S.; or the last surviving line of the CF du Calvados, closed for ever by the D-day invasion as its morning train stood ready to depart in Dives station. They also had—in retrospect—their mildly hilarious moments, like the sight of the long weekend 'convoys' on a line near Toulouse, ten or twelve packed coaches behind a wheezing 0-6-0T taking the inhabitants off for occasional recreation; or the sheer frustration confronting the lines in Dauphiné whose passengers might well have their papers demanded twice in a ten-mile run—once by the Gestapo and once by the local Maquis or Resistance fighters. However annoying to the enemy, it must have been frustrating too, if you were a local railway, to have your locomotives blown up on shed by over enthusiastic maquisards—and then have the one survivor smashed as well as soon as it returned home the next night. Such affairs did not really trouble the English minor lines since apart from the odd ones taken over to serve supply depots only one found itself right in the firing line. This, with typical English eccentricity, was one of the smallest of all, the 15-inch gauge Romney Hythe and Dymchurch Light Railway down by Dungeness. It not only got bombed and trampled on, it also was operated entirely by the military for nearly five years; it sported an armoured train equipped with machine guns and anti-tank rifles, and it carried much of the material for PLUTO—the Pipe Line Under The Ocean, through which flowed much of our forces' fuel supplies from late 1944 on. Unlike other military acquisitions it did *not* emerge from the war in better shape than it entered it.

Indeed very few major railways emerged in good shape. The British ones were exhausted by minimum maintenance, the continental ones suffered much from bombing and other depredations especially after the invasion of Europe in 1944. Then, if ever, they showed the vulnerability of rail transport to an enemy with air superiority. Whole German divisions being rushed forward by trains to conserve on wear and petrol found themselves strafed mercilessly by the Allied air forces, sidetracked by unco-operative railway men or halted time and time again as the Resistance blew up the track in front or behind them and then harrassed the stalled trains. Some units took literally weeks to cross France, arriving disorganised and often too late for the role assigned to them—supplies too were seriously held up, not only for the Germans but for the Allies. Some of the pre-invasion destruction took a long time to make good.

The end of World War 2 found European railways in a worse state than they had been in 1918. In Germany, worst hit of all, even coal trucks had to be pressed into use for emergency passenger services while trains of battered motley stock worked gingerly across temporary or heavily shored up engineering works. As after the earlier war, many of the best locomotives and vehicles were taken by the victors as reparations and once again German goods locomotives could be found scattered across the face of Europe. In fact the Kriegsloks sent to other countries outlasted those left in Germany itself.

In one way, however, the European continent found the destruction not an unmixed disaster. The railway system of Holland was so destroyed that the State Railways were able almost to start from scratch, electrifying where they chose and building new diesel stock for the rest. Holland was in 1956 one of the first European countries to dispense entirely with steam, while West Germany itself took advantage of its problems to create what is probably once again the most efficient railway in Europe (East Germany was another matter). All over the Middle East, railways took the opportunity to re-equip with ex-military stock—there are W.D. 2-8-0s puffing round Turkey to this day. France even went to the lengths of ordering a special new 'Austerity' 2-8-2 from the United States, the Class 141R which has been one of the most successful maids-of-all-work ever employed by the S.N.C.F. Ironically, it was probably the British railways that came off worst; they had not been greatly destroyed, just worked almost to exhaustion, and they were still under private ownership. Consequently they faced a long laborious period of patching up and making up general arrears of maintenance in an attempt to reach their former standards of excellence.

It is true to say that World War 2 is likely to be the last conflict in which railways were used extensively. The lessons it taught about their vulnerability under air and guerrilla attack, and the obvious successes of largely motorised armies, have led to a great decrease in their use for military purposes. All the minor conflicts since 1945 have emphasised that railways can only be used successfully with fairly static fronts and when running through friendly territory.

As a consequence, military interest has declined sharply and the military establishments in all countries—save possibly Russia, with her vast distances—have been run down. Many, like Longmoor in England, have even been closed as rail centres and it seems likely that they will not be reopened. The remaining railway troops will be trained mainly to operate existing lines if these are found viable during a campaign, and experiments with equipment are devoted to providing useful improvised stock to meet temporary needs. The day of the military railway is over.

THE COLOURED ILLUSTRATIONS

1 Palestine

2 Suez Canal defences

3 Map of Salonika

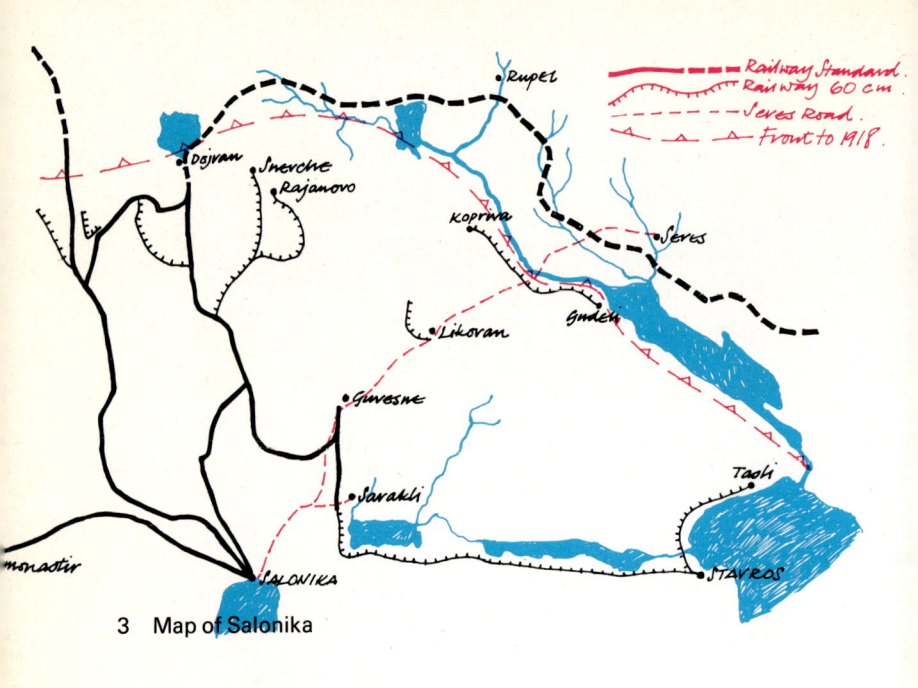

4 Mule train

5 Snevche Station

6 Stavros scene

7 Standard-gauge locomotive

9 Ardoviaduct

8   Train Dispatcher's Office

10　70cm gauge locomotive

11　Generator train

12 Büssing-NAG rail lorry

13 60cm gauge railway

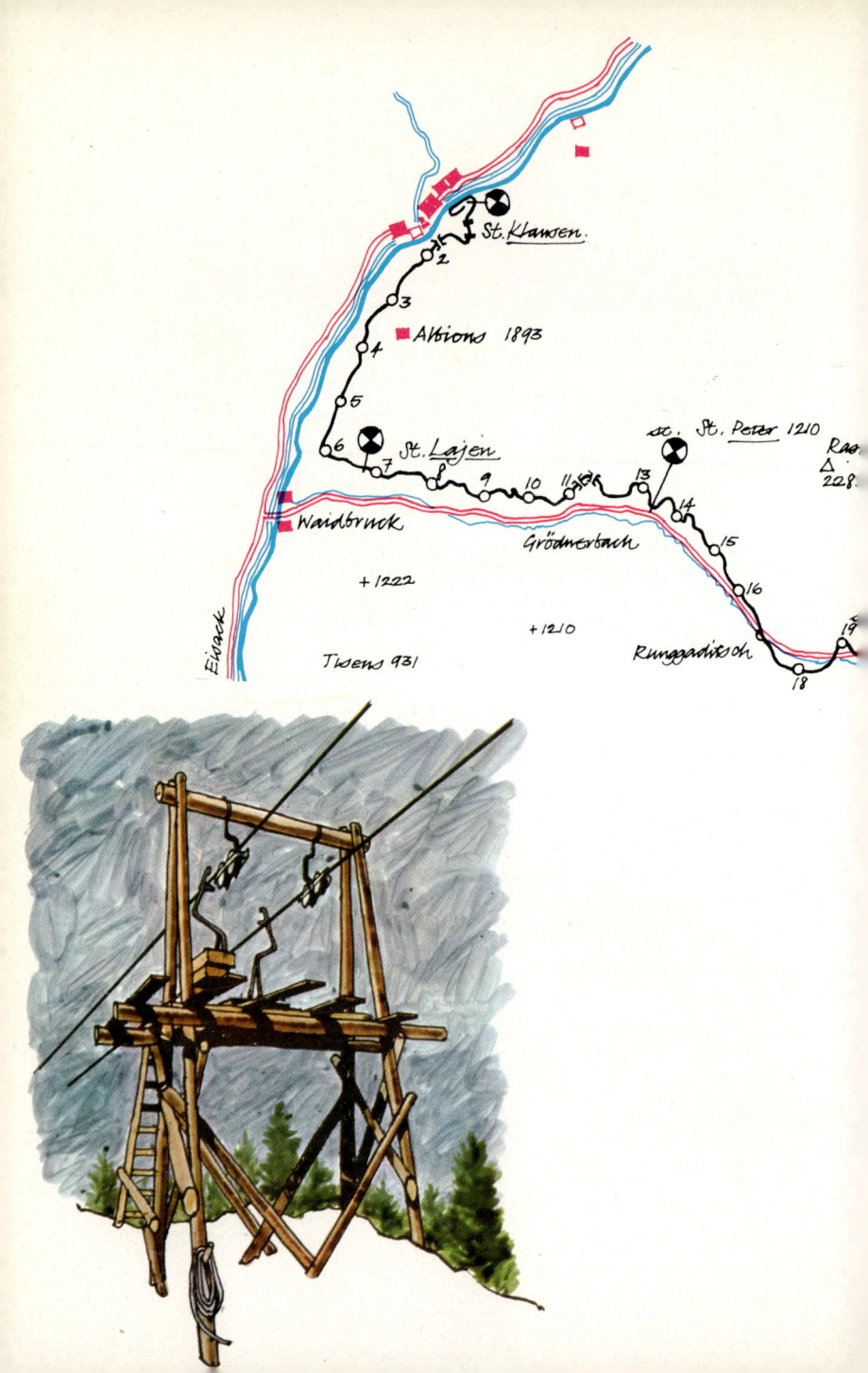

St. Klausen
Albions 1893
St. Lajen
Waidbruck
Grödnerbach
so. St. Peter 1210
Ras △ 228.
+1222
Eisack
Tisens 931
+1210
Runggaditsch

14   Grödnertal (Val Gardena) railway

15 Narrow gauge to Verdun

16 Voie sacrée

17 The reason why

18 Inspection

19 S.N.C.V. – Belgium: Type 21 Locomotive

20 Béthune train

21 Prussian P8

22 Prussian G8^1 0-8-0 (later DR C1.55)

23 Austrian armoured train, 1917-18

24 Russian armoured train, 1918-19

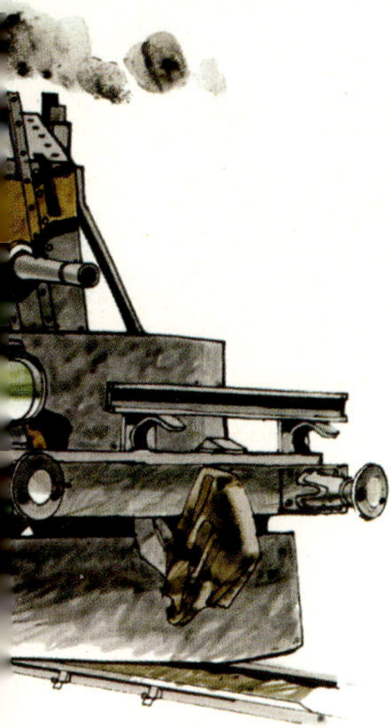

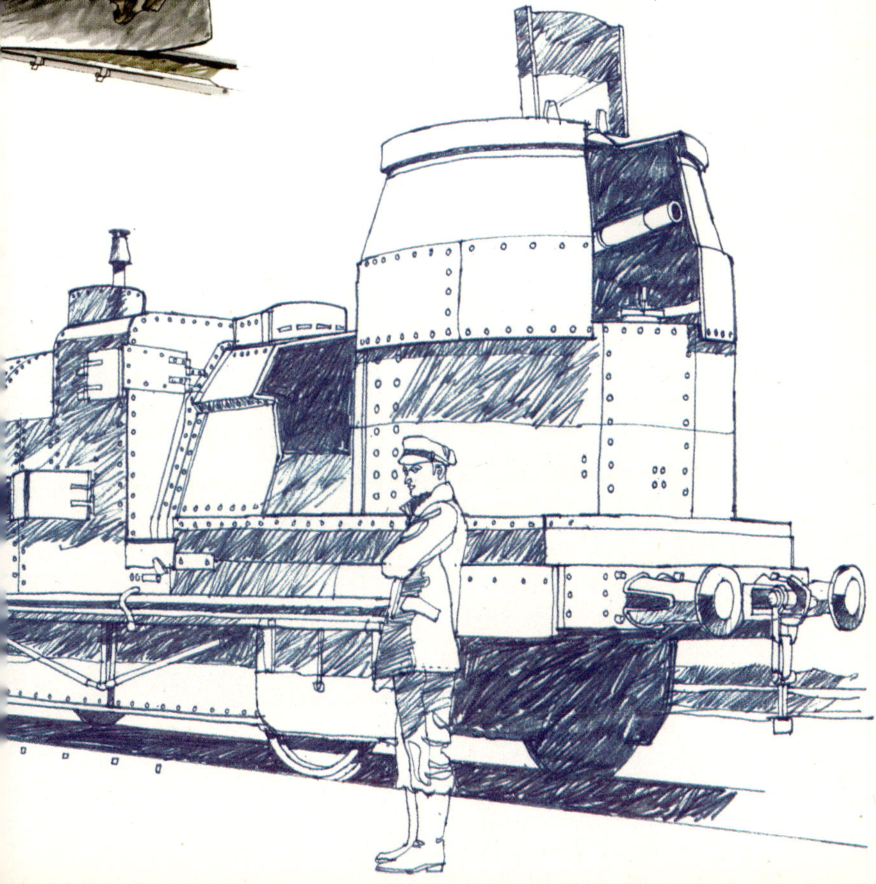

25 Decauville 0-6-0+0-6-0 for Morocco

27 L.M.R. breakdown crane

26 0-6-2T Thisbe

28 Farewell-1

29 Farewell-2

30 SG armoured train (G.B.)

31 Detail of gun-wagon (G.B.)

32 Narrow-gauge gun-wagon (G.B.)

33 British 9.2in rail-mounted gun for cross-Channel bombardment

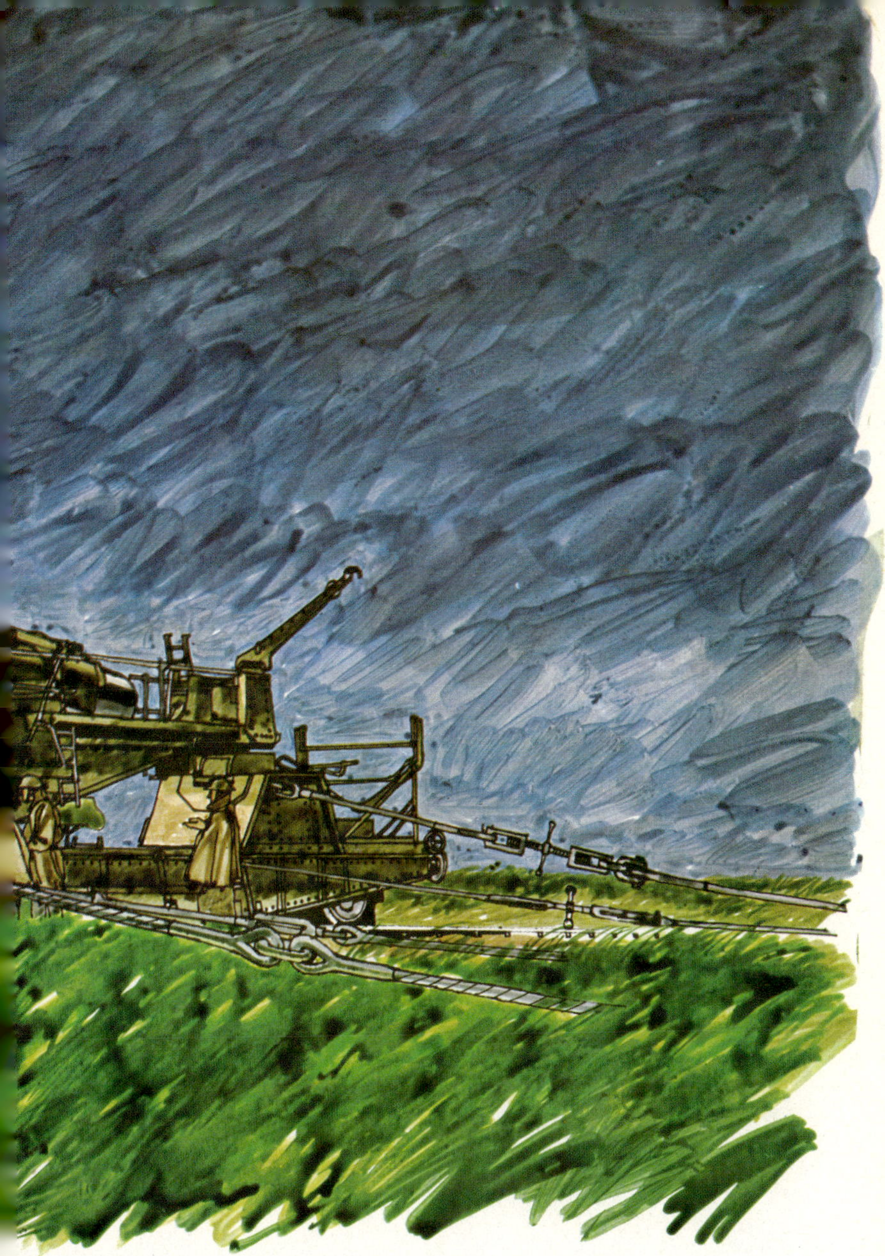

34 Class 44 – 2-10-0

35 Class 50 – 2-10-0

36 Class 52 – 2-10-0

37 Class 42 – 2-10-0

38 Class 52 Condensing Locomotive

39 Reichsbahn Class 03^{10} 4-6-2

40 Reichsbahn Class 94^1 0-10-0T

41 U.S. Army 2-8-0

42 Russian Army 2-8-0

43 Class B(5) 4-6-0

44 Class S (Cyrillic C) 2-6-2

45   Class Ye(E) 2-10-0

46   Dean Goods 0-6-0

47 Bulleid Q1 Class 0-6-0

48 British War Department 0-6-0ST

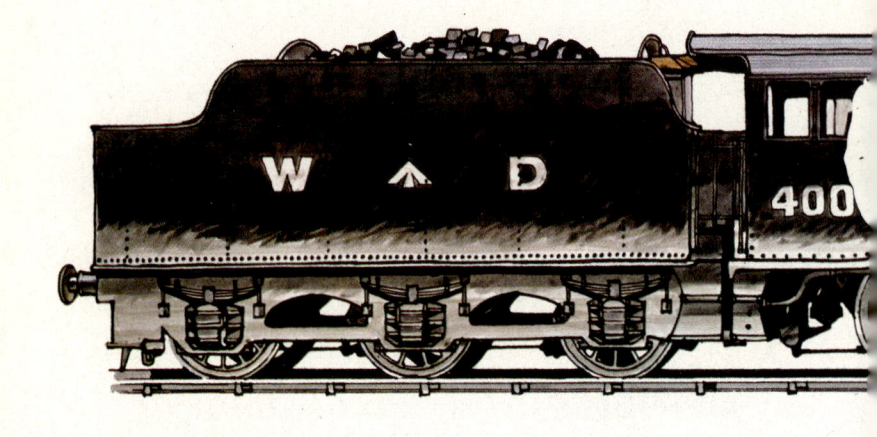

49 'Austerity' 2-8-0 (G.B.)

50 W.D. Standard 2-10-0

51 W.D. 2-8-0 armoured version

52 2-8-2+2-8-2 for Burma

53 4-8-2+2-8-4 for Kenya

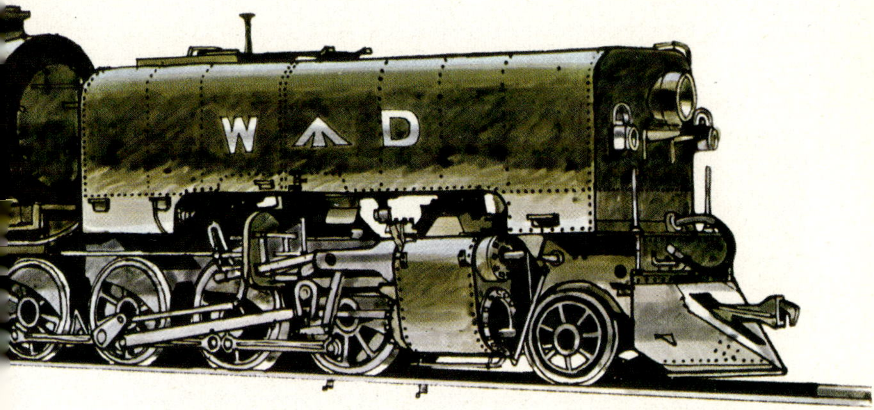
W D

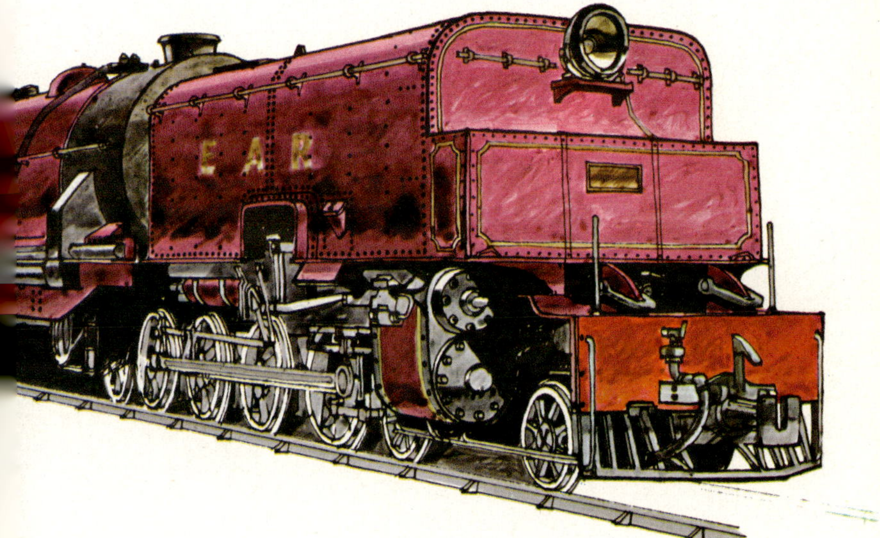
E A R

54 W.D. 0-6-0DE

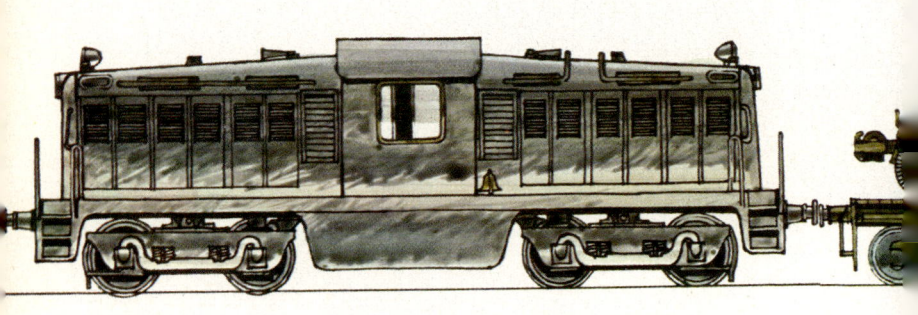

56 Whitcomb B-B (U.S.A.)

55 Wermacht 0-6-0DH

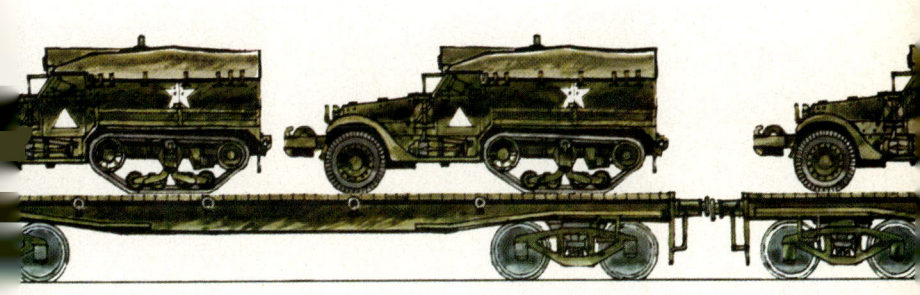

57 Build-up of locomotives

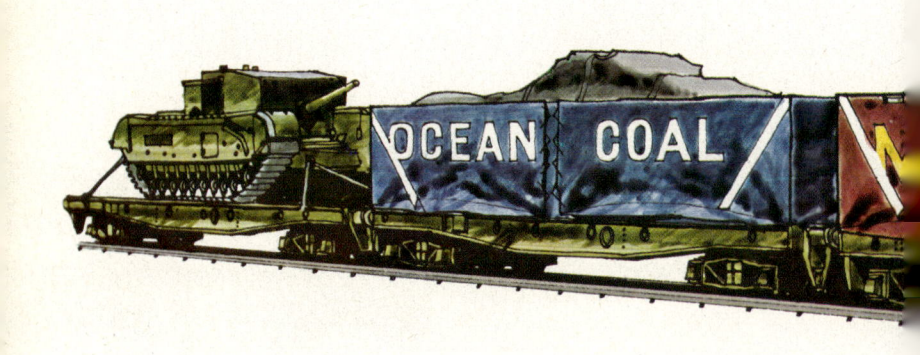

58 Tank trucks into coal wagons

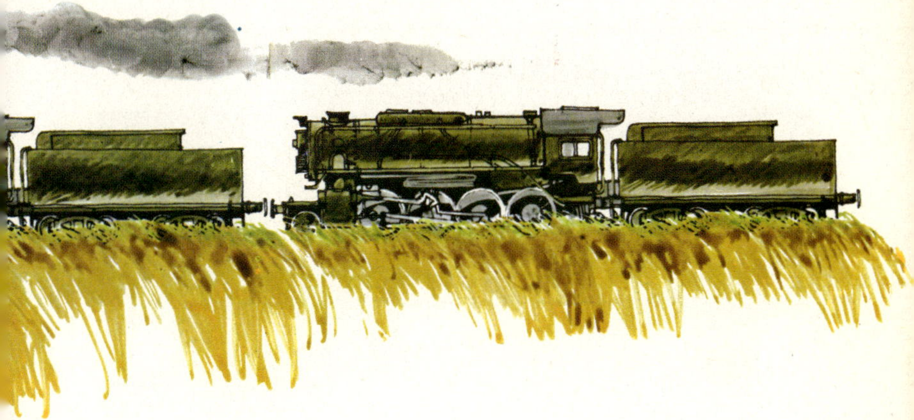

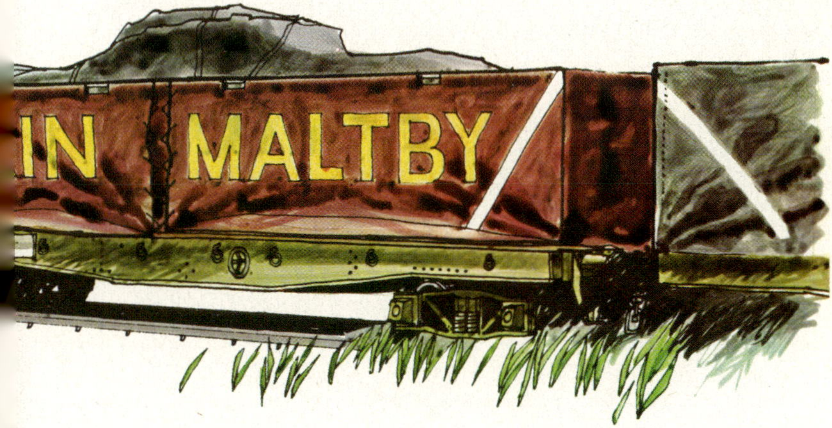
IN MALTBY

59 Concealed tank on wagon

60 El Alamein

61 Eritrea

62 First train Naples-Rome

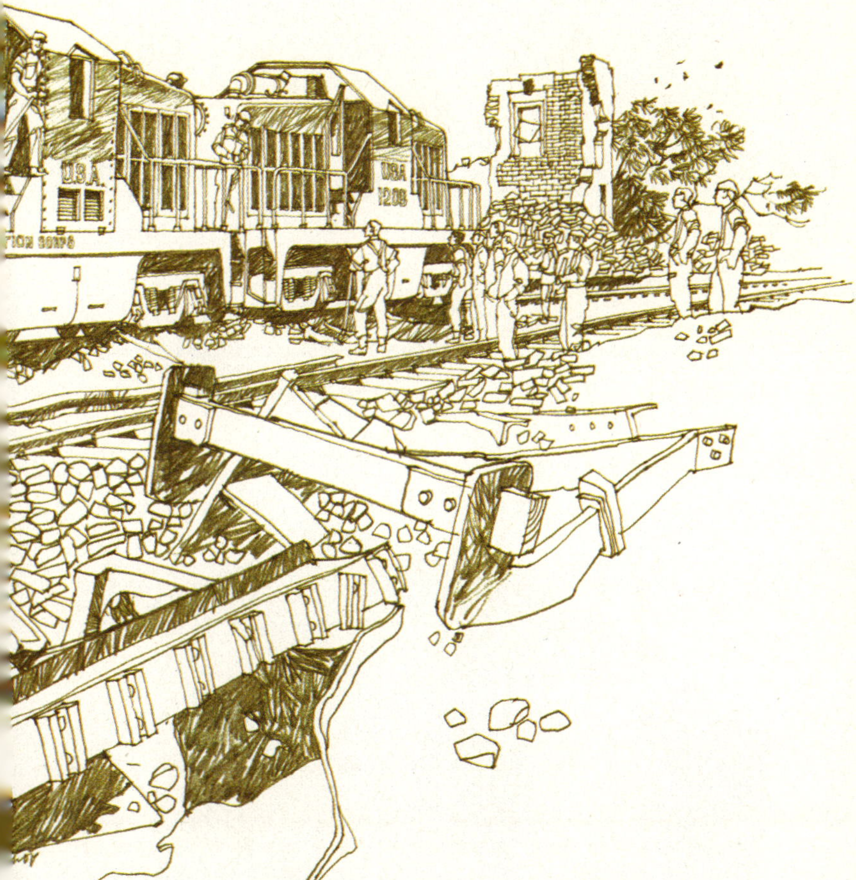
USA
USA

63/4 Russian armoured trains

65/6 Armoured wagons

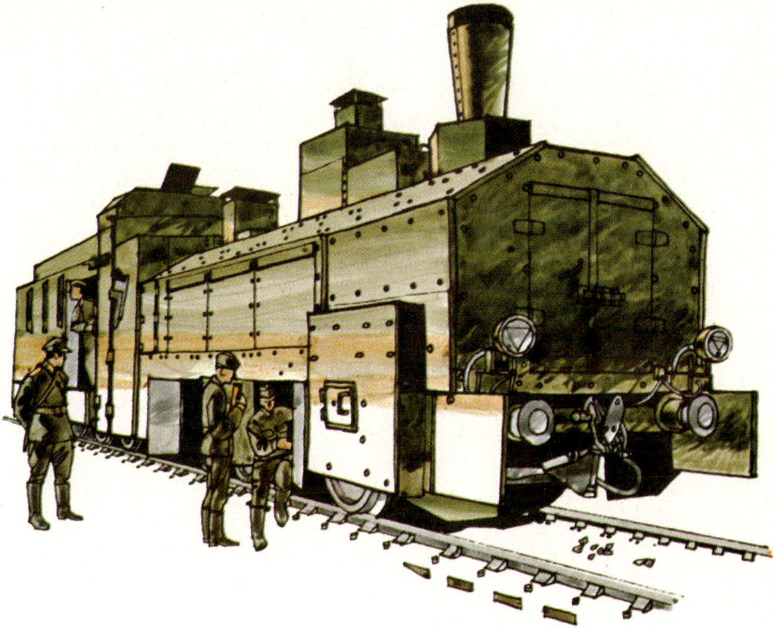

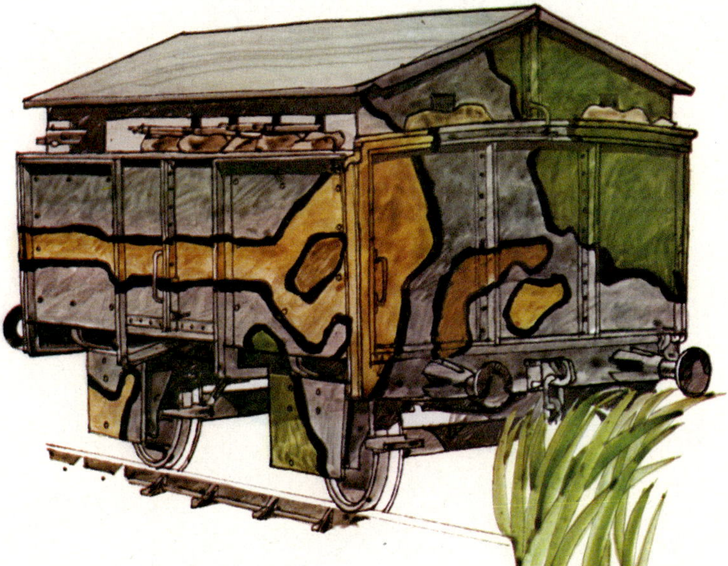

67 Sd Kfz 231 on rails

68 Czech armoured trolley

69 The bombing of Bielefeld

70 'Strafing an Emmett'

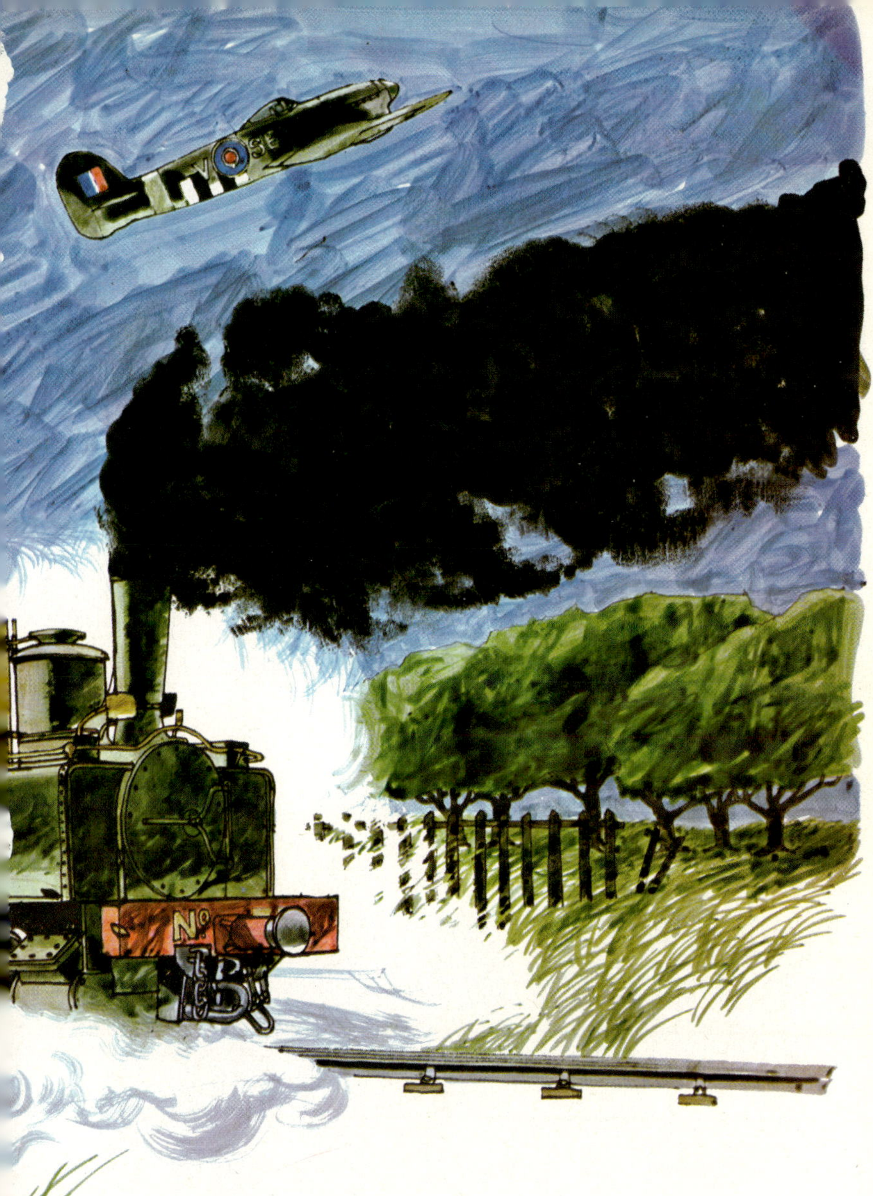

71 Smuggling

72 Revival in the Channel Isles

73 Heeresfeldbahn 0-8-0

74 Gazelle

75/76 Improvisation – 1

77 Improvisation – 2

78 Improvisation – 3

79 Railway loads

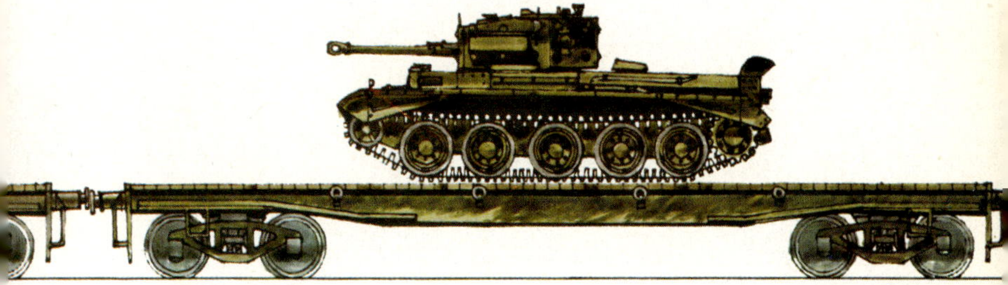

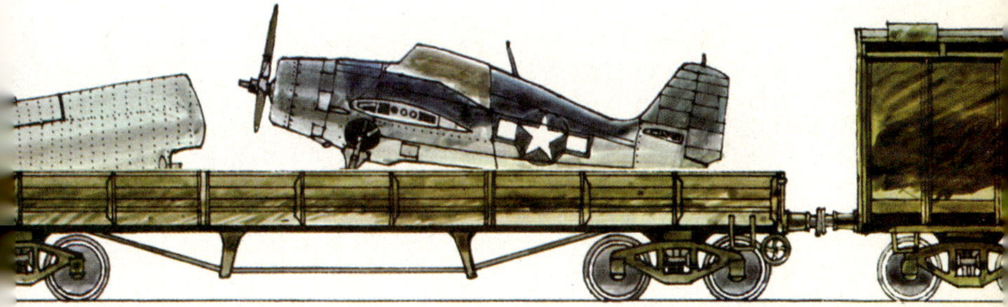

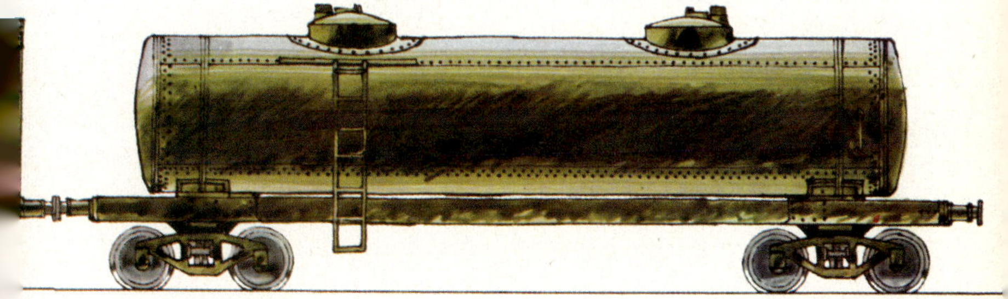

80 Railway loads

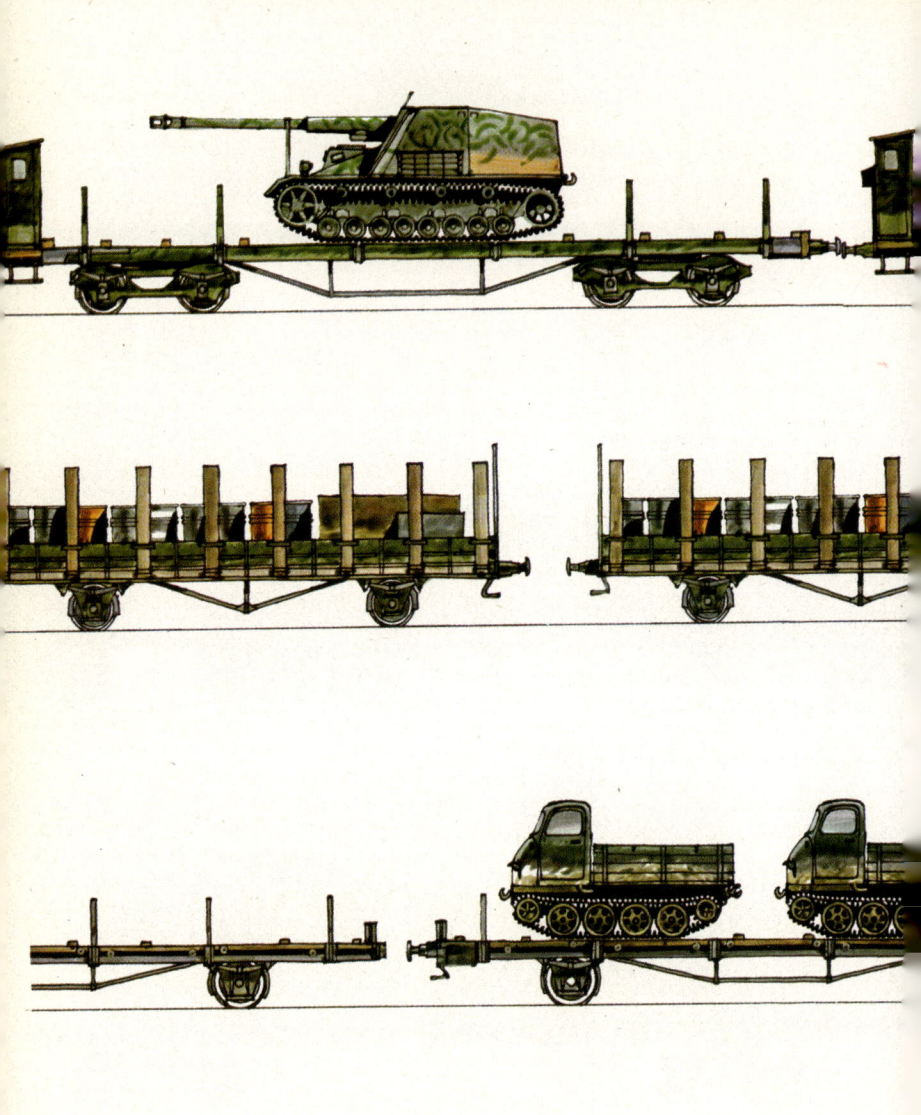

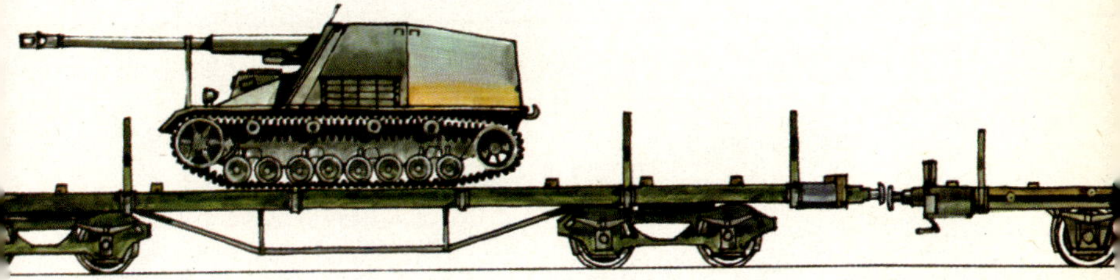

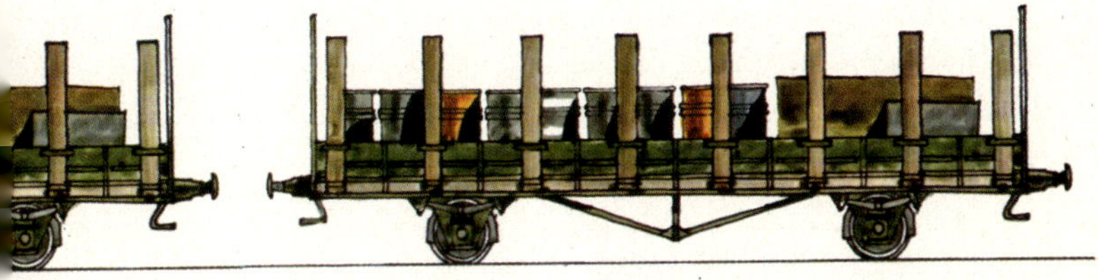

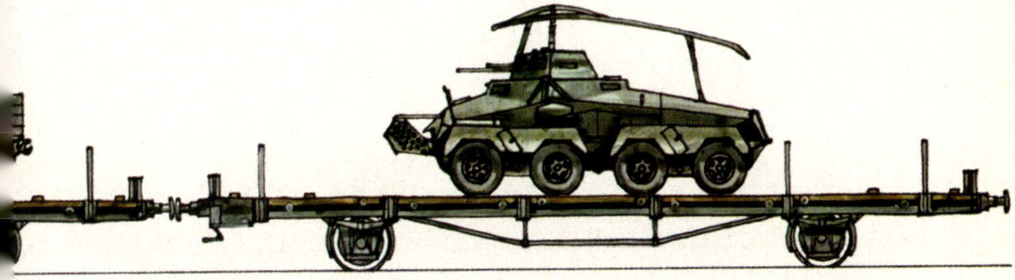

81 Rail by road

82 Road by rail

83 VIP load

84 Enemy load problems

85 Loading locomotives

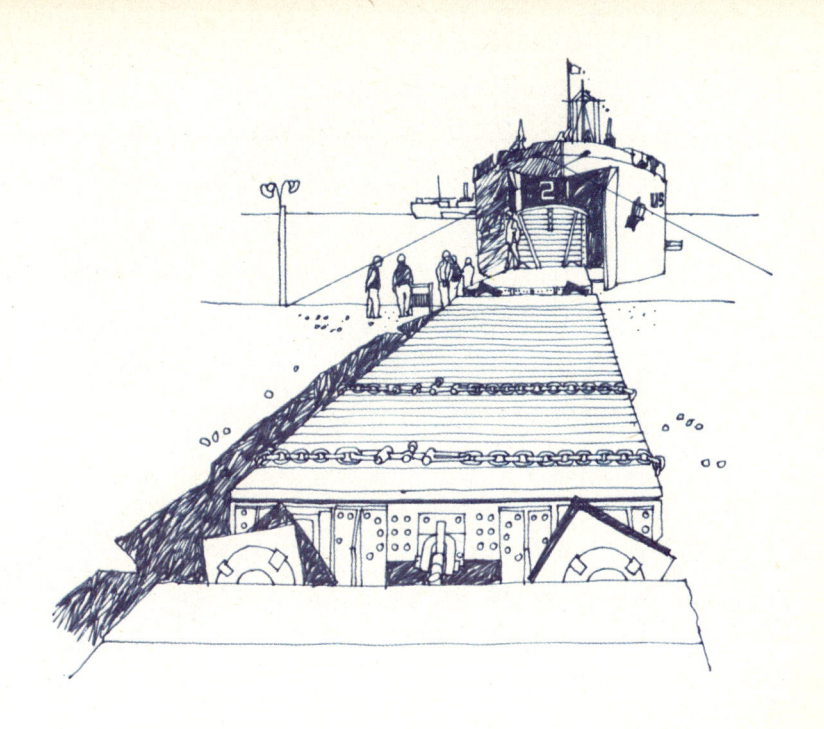

86/7 Loading rail vehicles onto LSTs

88 Approaching the 'hard'

89 Lowering the gantry platform

90 Aligning the drawbridge

91 Loading wagons

92/93 Quarter-ton truck convertible for rail use

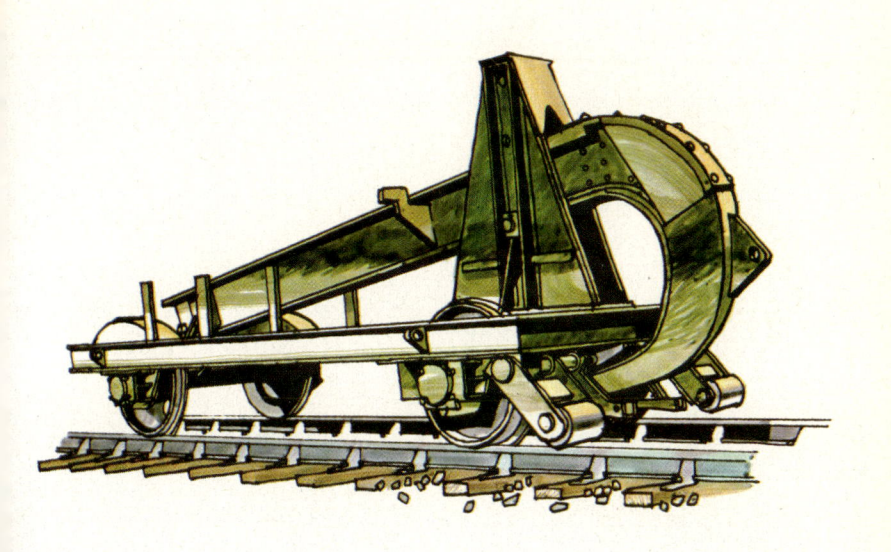

94/5 The hook

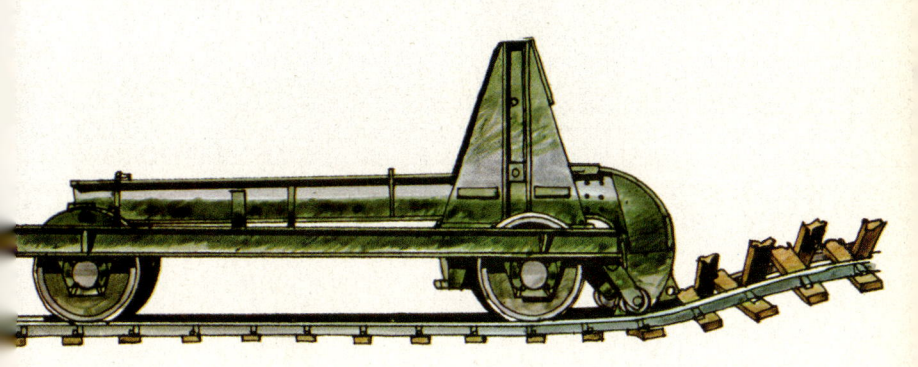

96 Panzer-carrying train

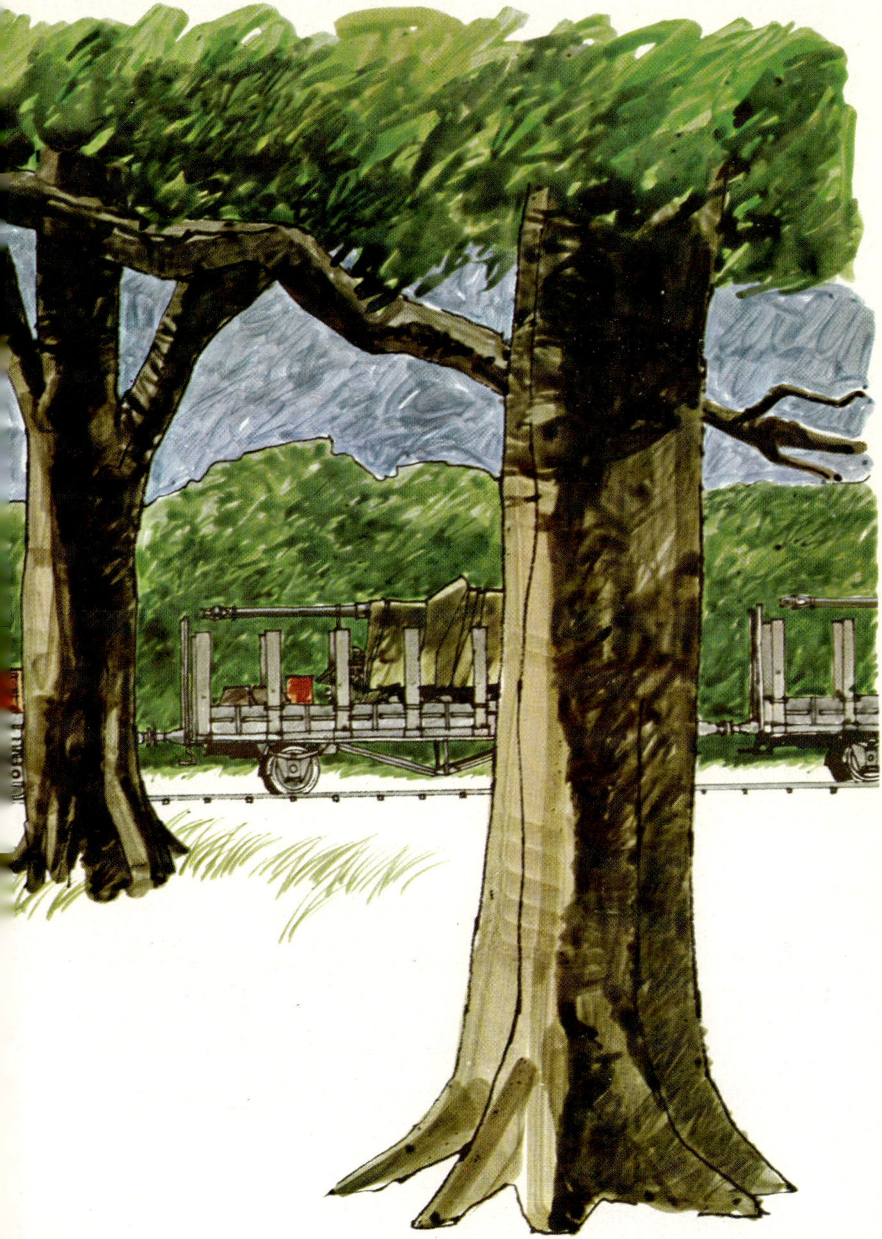

97 Tank-carrying truck

98 Armoured truck

99/100 Japanese armoured car on rails

101 Shaky rebirth

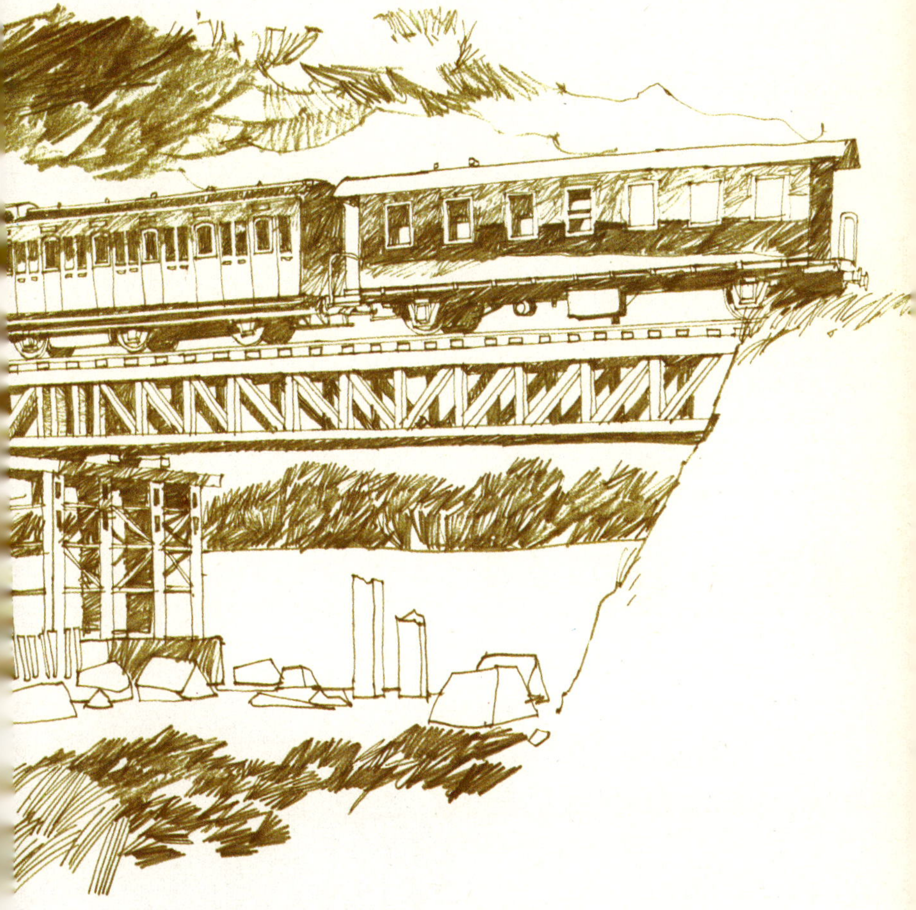

102 UNRRA 2-8-0

103 141R (S.N.C.F.)

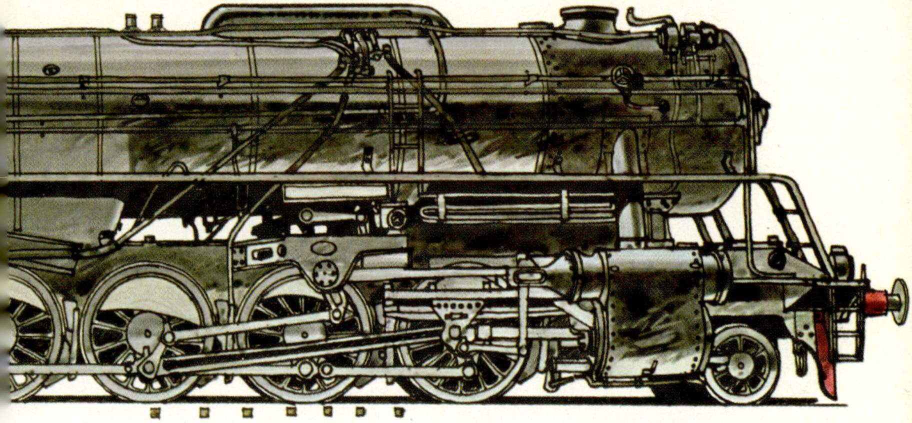

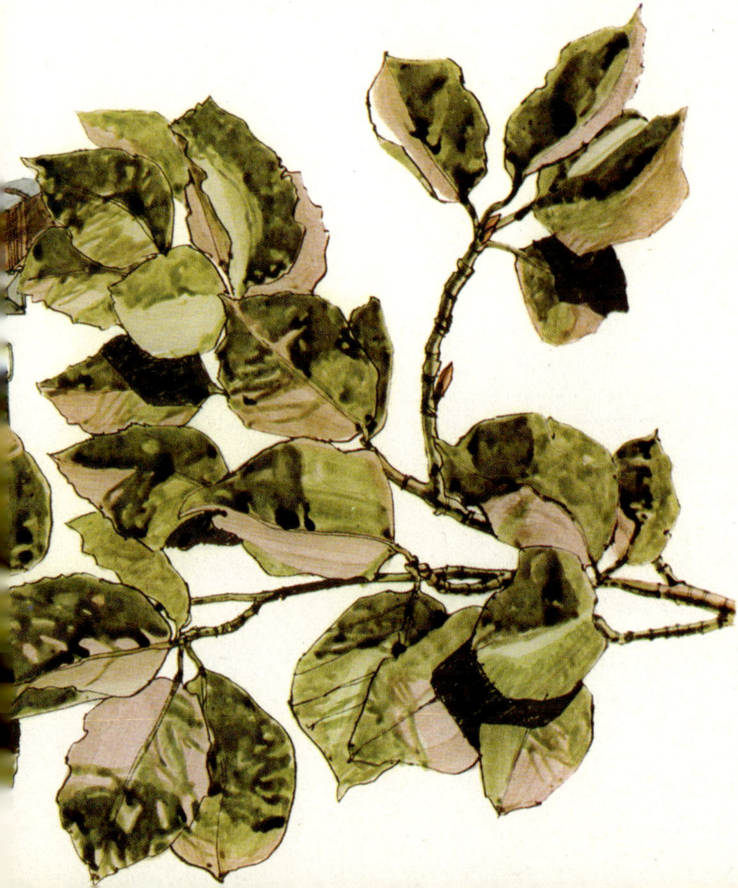

104 Bringing them back

105 The basic locomotive

106 S.N.C.F. version

107 British Railways

108 Yankee in Yorkshire

109 Land Rover road/railer

110 Land Rover: semi-permanent conversion

111 Ambush drill

112 Full circle

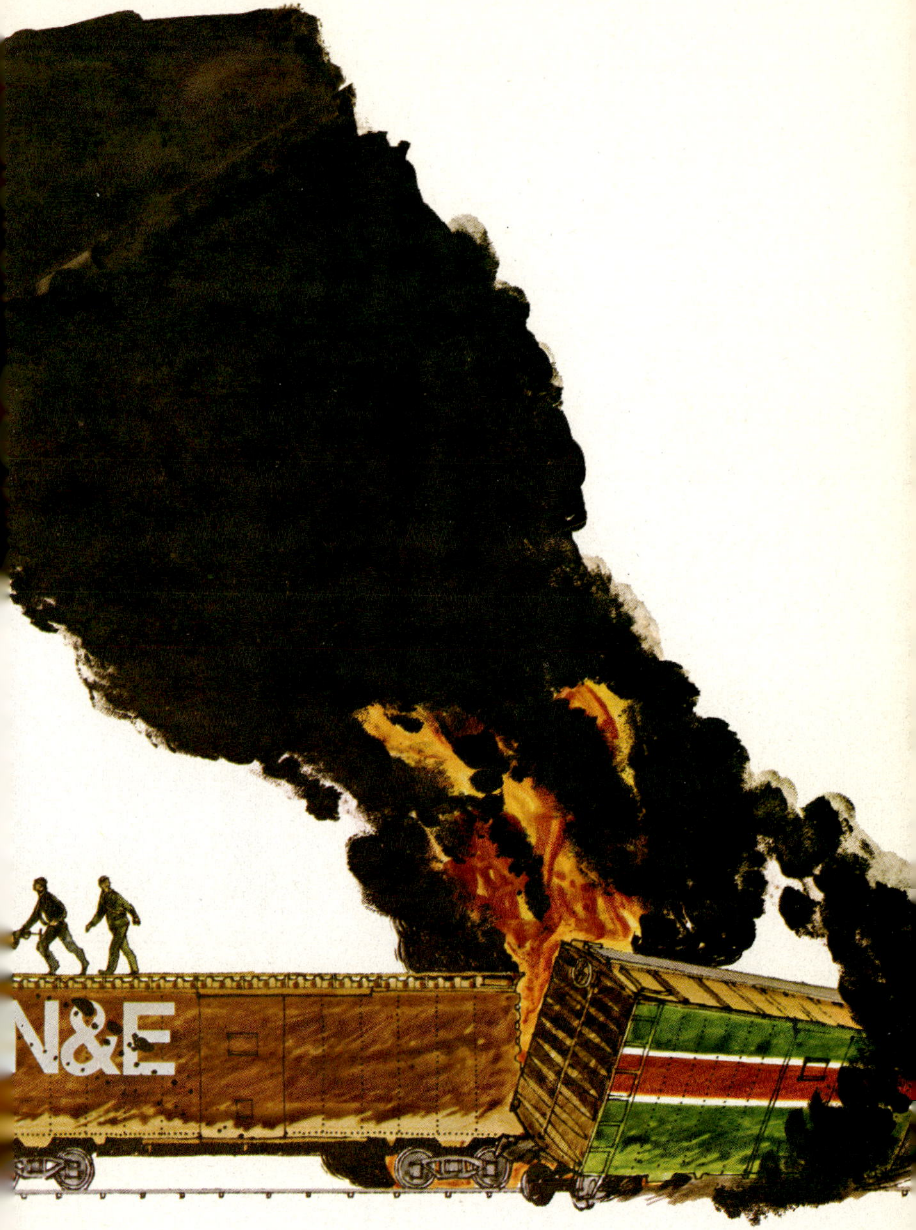
N&E

113 It'll never replace the train

DESCRIPTIVE NOTES

MINOR FRONTS

The previous volume ended officially in 1918 but lack of space forced omission of much that is of considerable interest. This volume, then, starts by describing some of the lesser known railway exploits of that war, especially those on the so-called minor fronts; Italy, the Middle East, Salonika. One could use page after page even in illustrating the activities of the smallest campaigns, though in most cases it was a matter mainly of impressing civilian railways and their stock. Perhaps the two following vignettes will pay tribute to the humdrum and unsung work of the many specially built lines that never saw a shot fired in anger—the railways on the lines of communication.

1 Palestine

A lively scene on one of the British 60cm gauge branches around Jaffa in Palestine, with Palestinian labour-corps recruits *en route* to Helmieh reception depot aboard a Baldwin-hauled train. The military signwriter seems to have had a nice sense of local colour in departing from the traditional lettering.

2 Suez Canal defences

A scene that portrays the essence of colonialism—British, French or German. It might be entitled 'the railway that never saw the war' for this is part of that 'complete 2ft 6in. gauge equipment' that the Royal engineers already had available in 1914. It failed to get to France, was sent out for use at Gallipoli but never reached there, and ended up by protecting the Suez Canal. The tractor is one of a series built before the war by Manning Wardle and the wagon a standard 'colonial' pattern vehicle of which examples were at work at Chattendon in Kent until the 1950s.

SALONIKAN EPISODE

Another front on which purpose-built military railways played an extended role was the rather odd affair in Salonika. This was quite typical of the 'forgotten' campaigns scattered around the Middle East, although its railway network was more extensive than most.

3 Map of Salonika

Basically the Salonika front came into being as a belated and rather desultory attempt to help Serbia against the Austrians and Bulgarians; the joint British and French force was beset from the start by indecision and lack of equipment so that a stalemate situation existed for most of the war. Railway facilities in that part of Macedonia were meagre in the extreme. To serve the western part, the allies had disconnected portions of three single track lines radiating from Salonika port on the standard gauge. One gave access to a rather unfriendly Greece, the others were truncated by the front itself and their railheads were under shellfire. In the north and east there was only the so-called Seres Road, originally fit only for mules, or supply by sea through the minute port of Stavros. Consequently in the same fashion as in Italy, spurs on the narrow gauge were built at various points to ease supply to

87

the front lines. They were all 60cm gauge, partly because some were originally provided by the French, partly because it took up less shipping space in the U-boat infested seas.

4 Mule train

Typical of the more minor 'capillaries' in the early days is this scene on the Mirova spur. At that time only a few French Decauville 0-6-0Ts and a handful of Hudson 0-6-0WTs (see Vol. I) were available as motive power and the more remote lines had to depend on mules. Three mules in tandem was the regular team for a 'C' class bogie wagon and for two or three four-wheelers; no doubt the semi-permanent nature of the railway and the flatter ground made for easier going than in France where a full artillery team of six were often harnessed to a single truck. Even so the driver's job cannot have been easy for few B or C class vehicles had pillar handbrakes; the only means of stopping was to thrust a sprag between the wheels or pin down the parking brake.

5 Snevche Station

Even on the dead-end spurs, proper termini were constructed, for the lines were worked as genuine railways. Snevche, on the French-built line from Sarigol, is a typical example, with its long covered storehouse—the sun could be very hot in a Macedonian summer. The layout, it will be noted, is typically French with a goods loop and run-round flanking the 'main-line' on either side.

6 Stavros scene

The major achievements of the Salonika campaign, however, were the two long 60cm gauge lines that could almost be classed as strategic railways. The Bulgars, with German assistance, built one down through the difficult Rupel Pass to supply their troops on the Struma. The British went even further, in 1918 constructing what was probably the most professional 60cm gauge railway of any combatant in the whole war. Stavros was a very unsatisfactory port—there were only three small ships and everything they brought had to be trans-shipped into lighters for onward transport. In consequence a complete railway, 93km long and equipped for full single-line working was built from Stavros to a standard-gauge railhead east of Salonika. Typical of its wayside stations was Planica, shown here with a heavily laden supply train crossing a light inspection car; for once the Crewe tractors could be put to good use!

A NEGLECTED FRONT

The use of railways on the major fronts in World War 1 is well known and has been duly catalogued in our first volume. Yet some of the 'minor' fronts had complicated railway nets although they are very little known; one such was the Austrian–Italian conflict in and around Sud-Tirol from 1915 to 1918.

The Austrian military railway service (Kaiserlich-Königlich Eishenbahntruppen) had already, by 1915, a long and distinguished history. Indeed the first light railway companies (Feldeisenbahnabteilungen) had been formed in 1873 and since 1883 had been amalgamated with telegraphist troops to form regiments. By 1914 there were two complete railway regiments in existence and a very careful study had been made of the conditions under which they would have to work. In particular the troops were trained in the construction and operation of lines in difficult country since all along the southern and western borders the land was mountainous. No less than four distinct categories of rail communication were envisaged and the appropriate material was available for all of them.

These categories were: standard gauge (like the Germans, the Austrian authorities had provision for military control of the civilian railways); Feldbahnen or field railways which were normally 60cm gauge, with standardised locomotives and stock; Rollbahnen or 'trolley lines' which were of 60cm gauge and which, despite their name, had both steam and motor locomotives; and seilbahnen or cable railways of which a considerable quantity were envisaged. In addition provision was made for using and extending other people's existing narrow-gauge lines, the Italians in particular being partial to these. The arrangement may be thought elaborate but to anyone knowing the Alpine valleys, the reasoning behind it is obvious. When the major Italo-Austrian front in the Dolomites became established it was normal practice for standard-gauge railheads to be miles from the front-line troops. From these railheads substantially engineered 70/76cm gauge lines had to be built up narrow twisting valleys to reach the high plateaux and from these in turn stemmed the final stage: the rollbahnen, or, when even these could progress no further, the cable suspension lines which could jump across valleys and climb at steep angles. No doubt these would have been even more used except that in their primitive form they were not adapted for passenger traffic and their freight-carrying capacity was small even compared with a 60cm gauge line.

The Austro-Hungarian army was fighting constantly in Sud-Tirol from 1915 to 1918 and during much of that time the front remained fairly static. In consequence several very substantial narrow-gauge railways were put into service, either built new or partly reconstructed from former Italian lines and these were taken over by the Italians after the war, surviving as civilian railways into the 1950s and 1960s. Notable were the spectacular Grödnertalbahn, Fliemstalbahn and Dolomitenbahn, the two latter of which were in later days electrified.

7 Standard-gauge locomotive

For the massive quantity of supplies needed, the standard-gauge railways were upgraded and, in places, extended. Locomotives were requisitioned from, or allocated for use by, the civilian companies, notably the M.A.V. (Hungarian railways) and the Austrian Sudbahn (Southern Railway), a big private concern that served much of the south. Typical of the locomotive types in use is this heavy freight 2-8-0, designed for the Sudbahn and kk Staatsbahn by the famous Karl Gohlsdorf as Sudbahn Class 170. A distinctive Austrian feature is the prominent steampipe connecting its twin domes. The locomotive is shown testing a provisional bridge and in reality the picture could be a view of almost anywhere—the class lasted in service with the Austrian state railways as Cl.56 until well after World

War 2, and in 1973 a few were even then in use by the private Graz-Koflacher Eisenbahn. Main dimensions were: length *c.* 11·02m; coupled wheel diameter 1·3m; weight in working order 68t.

8 Train Dispatcher's Office

Operation, at least on the more important lines, was by the normal method of Fahrdienstleitung (traffic control) then in use on the Austrian civilian railways. This was designed for single-line working and involved dividing the line into sections. The ends of each section were stations which contained a traffic office (not a signal-box) in telegraphic communication with its neighbours. Trains were dispatched from station to station using train-orders and telephones to ensure that only one train was in a section at any one time. This rather charming scene shows a typical office. On the left and right backgrounds are officers contacting the next offices 'up' and 'down' the line; on the left is a clerk making up the train register, while the Fahrdienstleiter himself—with officer rank—supervises all with a steely eye.

9 Ardoviaduct

Besides the material and operating aspects the Austrians were, like others, greatly concerned with construction. They had special railway construction companies and, since they expected to operate in difficult country where railways were vulnerable, they had standard temporary bridging equipments. Most massive was the Roth-Waagner bridge, an equipment that could be constructed to a maximum height of 50 metres, a maximum single span of 70 metres and to carry a maximum axle-load of 20 tonnes. Some 2,667 metres (nearly 1½ miles) worth were built. More common, however, was the lighter Kohn-Brückengerät (Kohn-system bridging apparatus) devised by a Hungarian engineer of that name. This could take a maximum axle-load of 15 tonnes and a maximum single span of 45 metres—over 5,300 metres-worth were supplied! It could be used singly or in multiple and the plate shows a typical multiple application. This is a military bridge replacing the five-span Ardoviaduct on the Piave Valley line after the latter was blown up by retreating Italians. It comprises components of four Kohn girder spans with three Kohn-type metal piers socketed into steel foundations—and was built in two and a half months between December 1917 and February 1918. The problem was complicated by the fact that only an isolated section of the Piave Valley line was available to the Austrians so that all material had to be brought from Toblach over narrow-gauge lines and cable railways—the 'permanent' narrow-gauge Dolomitenbahn south from Toblach had not then been finished.

FELDBAHNEN

10 70cm gauge locomotive

Most substantial of the standardised equipments were those provided for the 70cm gauge Feldbahnen—and in slightly modified form for some of the 76cm gauge permanent railways that were built. This shows the standard eight-coupled locomotive of Class 3, of which some sixty were built before and during the war. With an all-up weight of only 12·6 tonnes the locomotive could run over quite lightly laid lines; the provision of 'all-wheels coupled' gave good adhesion and the extra tender enabled a plentiful supply of fuel and extra water to be carried without overloading the locomotive. The basic machine was a well-tank locomotive and the tender was by no means obligatory neither was the spark-arrestor. The various machines differed in detail according to their 'mark no', Reihe IIIc (Class 3c) in particular having a much more modern cab and neater side-bunkers.

11 Generator train

A rather less conventional device, was the so-called 'Generator-zug' built in both standard- and narrow-gauge versions and, originally, at least, capable of being converted to run on either road or rail. The 'locomotive' or 'tractor' of this formidable-looking equipment was in fact just what its name implied—a mobile petrol-electric generating plant. It was capable only of propelling itself but each of the specially built trailers had an electric motor or motors fed from the generator by a single cable running right along the 'train'.

The narrow (70cm) gauge version was a rather crude development of some even cruder 'feldbahnbenzintriebwagen' (petrol railcars) built on wagon chassis. It has a 100-hp petrol engine coupled to a 300-V, 13-amp generator, was designed to 'tow' up to twenty-five bogie wagons each fitted with one belt-driven motor and could carry up to 90 tonnes—not a bad loading considering the gradients.

The standard-gauge version shown in the plate was considerably more elaborate. The Generator-car was purpose-built and could tow five wagons on the road and ten on rails; conversion took about forty minutes. The 150-hp petrol engine was coupled to a 300-V d.c. generator and powered two electric motors on each vehicle; final drive was by spur gearing to one axle. The whole thing appears rather cumbersome but in practice was reasonably effective in the hilly conditions prevailing.

12 Büssing-NAG rail lorry

The Austrian army was, in any case, very fond of convertible vehicles. More information is now available about the rail lorry mentioned briefly in our previous volume and this plate shows one in use on a standard-gauge branch. It was a normal 35-hp four-cylinder Fross-Büssing road lorry provided as standard with railway couplings and having four forward speeds and one reverse. Conversion involved replacing the road wheels with steel rail-wheels and locking the front axle rigid, a process that was supposed to take about one hour. In its rail form the lorry could tow a trailer and between them they could carry a total of ten tons—but with only a hand-brake, and with no synchromesh on the gearbox this must have resulted in some tricky situations on the steeper side-lines!

13 60cm gauge railway

Smallest and lightest of the conventional railways were the 60cm rollbahnen which served as feeders to the front-line troops where the terrain allowed. As with allied light railways in similar situations, these might be powered with horses, crude petrol tractors, small industrial-type steam locomotives or larger six- and eight-coupled machines of German feldbahn pattern. Wagon stock was mainly fairly crude four-wheelers although a surprising quantity of semi-open toastrack coaches were also provided; the reason was that even the 60cm lines were often ten or more km in length and so regular passenger services were provided.

14 Grödnertal (Val Gardena) railway

In and around the Dolomites the Austrian authorities built no less than three substantially engineered 76cm gauge railways that were in all respects the equal of similar civilian lines elsewhere. Indeed one, the extensive and magnificently engineered Fleimstalbahn (Auer-Predazzo) with its specially built 2-6-6-0 Mallet tanks took nearly two years to build, and included no less than fourteen major bridges and six tunnels in its 50km. But both it and the spectacular Dolomitenbahn from Tolbach were converted to metre gauge by the Italians after the war and electrified. Far better known, since it retained steam traction right up to closure in 1960 was the Grödnertal line from Klausen (now Chiusa) to Plan 44km away in the high Dolomites.

Just because it was never electrified, one should not consider the Grödnertal/Val Gardena railway as of less interest than the others. Even those who never got beyond its lower terminus could have a foretaste of what they missed for the line had to curve round in a complete circle, over a long viaduct just to get away from the junction station, and it had already passed through two tunnels before it finally disappeared from sight into its private valley. Indeed it was mainly the restricted loading gauge caused by its heavy earthworks that prevented later closure and regauging. As with the Fleimstal railway a special locomotive class was provided to work the line. Class K, built by Krauss, Linz in 1916, was officially a 'Zwillingslok' designed to work in pairs but was often used singly. It was an 0-8-0T with Klien-Lindner articulation on the leading and trailing coupled axles, a length of 7·05 metres and a weight in working order of 27·5 tonnes. The line served hospitals in the valley and a tangle of interconnecting cableways springing from its terminus at Plan; several of these had 'branch lines' and there were even branches off the branch lines in one or two cases. Certainly the railway was busy, with trains running in 'processions' twice or thrice daily. The planned 700 tonne daily capacity was fully needed.

After the war the thrifty Italian victors did not dismantle the railway but took it over, complete with original stock. For many years it served the locality, briefly returning to its old role from 1939 to 1945 carrying wounded to the numerous hospitals and sanitoria. It finally succumbed to road transport in 1960, when the original K class 0-8-0T were still puffing valiantly up and down.

THE RAILWAYS AT VERDUN

Perhaps the Epochal battle of World War 1, at least for the French was the holocaust of Verdun, which between 1916 and 1918 accounted for many thousands of both German and French casualties. Both sides indeed suffered to an extent that virtually diminished their effectiveness for the rest of the war and the battle undoubtedly led the French to their later 'Maginot Line' policy.

In summary the fortifications of Verdun were sufficiently strong to defeat the attacker; it was the human element that was likely to break and its strength was maintained only by the ability of the defenders to transport the huge quantities of supplies and to relieve the battered troops constantly with fresh drafts. The transport system best known is the notorious 'Voie Sacrée', the single main road along which a nose-to-tail stream of lorries poured for twenty-four hours of the day; the railways which made just as great a contribution are virtually ignored yet without them Verdun would have fallen.

15 Narrow gauge to Verdun

Most obscure of all the transport routes was that of the local metre gauge departmental concern the 'Compagnie Meusienne' twisting and turning across the countryside in true light railway fashion; its routes nevertheless reached right into Verdun town itself and during the crucial first few weeks of June its use virtually saved the situation. Though later cut back, it was quickly taken over by the military and up to the end carried a substantial proportion of the more mundane supplies such as rations and forage. Some 800 vehicles and seventy-five locomotives were brought in from other French light railways causing fantastic complications because their couplings, brake-lines and even solebar heights were often incompatible; furthermore a train of such motley stock could take perhaps only a quarter of the load of a standard-gauge train. None the less by running what amounted to 'merry-go-round' trains of fixed rakes, and by reorganising the major trans-shipment points it was possible to operate up to thirty-four trains a day. Symbolic is this ambulance train, often carrying over 800 wounded daily. The track is Meusienne, the 4-6-0T locomotive comes from the CF du Sud de la France, the front coach from an Économiques line, the van from a branch of the CF Departementaux.

16 Voie Sacrée

Alongside the hopelessly overloaded Meusienne ran the nearest road equivalent to a railway that has ever been— the notorious Voie Sacrée. This narrow French 'chaussée' has passed into history as the road that needed a man a metre to maintain—and which must have killed almost the same number in accidents and strain. It was no wonder when one considers the constant stream of solid-tyred petrol lorries which mercilessly ground its surface to pieces almost as quickly as it could be made-up. Nearly 50,000 vehicles were eventually collected from all over France to keep this route running.

17 The reason why

All this trouble was caused because the former Est railway line from the north-west was made unusable by German shelling well before the battle started. Scenes like these soon convinced the French of the hopelessness of running supply trains in even at night but with Teutonic thoroughness they were not given time to provide an effective substitute before the battle started. It was not until the main attack had been held that in the spring of 1917 a completely new standard-gauge railway was thrust in from the south-west as far as Dugny (60km) whence it could connect to an existing line. This was able to take much of the load off the Voie Sacrée, although the Meusienne continued in full use.

18 **Inspection**

Symbolic of the importance of Verdun to the French High Command is this picture of the then C-in-C Marshall Joffre and Army commander General Foch disembarking from a special train on the new line at Souilly behind Verdun; presumably arriving on a visit of inspection it was a clear testimony to the railways that they obviously found it convenient not to transfer to road transport until the last moment. One assumes their empty cars had had to brave the dust, fumes and bumps of the Voie Sacrée to meet up with them.

CIVILIAN SECONDARY RAILWAYS ON THE WESTERN FRONT

We cannot leave World War 1 without some mention of the more specialised aspects of railway work that occurred in its later stages. Notable among the absence so far is any mention of the part played by civilian systems that happened to be caught in the battle zones on the Western Front.

19 **S.N.C.V.—Belgium: Type 21 Locomotive**

Biggest and most squarely caught were the extensive metre-gauge lines of the Belgian Secondary Railways Company (S.N.C.V. or Societé des Chemins de Fer Vicinaux). These were virtually cut in two by the northern front; those in German territory closed or carried on as best as they could. In the triangle of Belgium left to the allies, things were slightly different. With considerable foresight the Baron Empain, director of the big coastal group, had arranged to collect much of its equipment at the western end and this was immediately made available. To operate it a military Section Vicinale des Chemins de Fer (S.V.C.F.) was formed, composed almost entirely of S.N.C.V. employees called up into the reserve. Its work is not much known since for the most part it operated in support of the small Belgian army but, like other railways, it acquired a number of 'standard' locomotives from allied sources.

Most effective were some British built 0-6-0Ts later taken into S.N.C.V. stock as the Type 19. Slightly more exotic were twenty 0-6-0 tram engines built by the American Locomotive Company in 1915. These were officially intended to be like the others but for some reason—perhaps the shape of the side tanks—they had a distinctly American flavour. They were subsequently taken into S.N.C.V. stock as 1001–20 but were never regarded with much favour. Their weight of 26·5 tonnes made them rather heavy on the track. Leading dimensions were: length 7·29m; wheelbase 1·98m; coupled wheel diameter 865mm; cylinders 290 by 406mm.

20 **Béthune train**

Typical of the individual local companies swallowed by the war was the CF de l'Artois, an amiable concern in northern

94

France joining Béthune to Estaires on the metre gauge. The advent of war saw the company abruptly jolted out of its usual calm, all services being suspended on 25 August 1914 'due to the advance of German forces'. When the front stabilised the line was about 10km behind the allied lines and parallel to them. Very restricted services were restarted in January 1915 with a much reduced personnel; the line and its material were damaged several times in bombing raids and had to be helped out by a French Engineer detachment before finally closing on 16 November 1916. On that day it was taken over entirely by the British Army who worked it intensively until 1918 with the original stock and whatever else they could lay their hands on. Overrun during the big German offensives of 1918, the railway was badly damaged both during that fighting and during the subsequent German retreat. The line was so worn out by 1919 that it did not reopen even partially until late in 1920; even then much of the stock had to be renewed and the final section from La Gorgue to Estaires did not recommence operations until nearly nine years later. The story is a microcosm of the effect of war on railways unfortunate enough to be caught up in it.

GERMAN STANDARD-GAUGE WAR LOCOMOTIVES

Not so far mentioned were the German equivalents of the allied war locomotives. With considerable thoroughness the German State Railways, and particularly the Prussian ones, had planned their requirements to coincide with those of the military. The old joke that German engines were always built with an eye on other people's loading gauges was not far from the truth. Certainly the funnels were in two pieces so that the top half could be quickly unbolted, and the cab roof could also be lowered on some big machines.

21 Prussian P8

Perhaps the most famous of all the German general-purpose locomotives was the Prussian P8 class 4-6-0 (later DR & DB Class 38). An excellent maid-of-all-work, this surprisingly handsome machine was built in great numbers from 1906 onwards. The Prussian railways alone had 3,370 examples by 1918 and even after extensive dispersal of the class as 'reparations' after the war, the newly formed Reichsbahn had well over 2,000 in service. The locomotive was so simple, rugged and effective that it was again chosen as an interim 'standard' type in 1924 and the Reichsbahn ended up with no less than 3,052 of them. The last ones did not retire from service until 1973, so they played their part in two world wars. Main dimensions were: length 18·59m; boiler pressure 12 atm; cylinders 575 × 630mm; weight in working order 78·2t. At various times both cylindrical tank and conventional tenders were fitted and the class could be seen both with and without smoke deflectors of different types.

22 Prussian G8¹ 0-8-0 (later DR Cl.55)

Goods equivalent of the P8 were the G8 and G8¹ 0-8-0 locomotives. Originally designed in 1902, the original G8 gave way in 1913 to the G8¹ of which some 5,000 were built. As with the P8, the class lasted right into the 1970s with the

East and West German railways and was a straightforward rugged design. It was much coveted by the victor countries as a 'reparations' engine and examples could be seen all over Europe until recently. The example shown is in the livery of the S.N.C.B.—the Belgian National Railways. Main dimensions were: (G8¹) length 18·29m; boiler pressure 14 atm; cylinders 600 × 660mm; weight in working order 69·9t.

ARMOURED TRAINS AGAIN

23 Austrian armoured train, 1917-18

By and large World War 1 did not offer the same opportunities for armoured train work as had, for example, the Boer War. The one possible exception was in central Europe where the Austro-Hungarian forces fought a rambling war of movement with the Russians, switching back and forth across the southern steppes. Not a great deal is known in detail about the trains employed but certainly this rather primitive one did exist. It was standard gauge and consisted of one fully armoured locomotive coupled between four-wheeled wagons, with a further locomotive at the rear end. The forward gun wagon mounted a light quick-firer—probably the continental equivalent of a two-pounder—and both had armoured fighting compartments with gun ports each side for small arms fire. The whole was surmounted by an armoured conning tower. What appears to be an armoured ammunition wagon was coupled behind the centre locomotive.

24 Russian armoured train, 1918-19

Even less is known about this armoured train of 1918 vintage used by the Tsarist General Semenoff in an ineffective fight against Bolsheviks in Siberia. Whether specially built or 'reclaimed' from the Austrian front, it was a very elaborate affair with an 0-8-0 tender locomotive coupled between long gun trucks. The front truck had two elaborate cupolas, apparently able to revolve and mounting a field gun; various flaps and ports were provided along with a commander's pedestal. Behind the locomotive was a truck with an armoured ammunition or fighting compartment leading into a more simple, open-topped turret mounting a light quick-firing gun. Like all armoured trains it was very vulnerable to mobile troops and was apparently something of a white elephant.

MORE COLONIAL RAILWAYS

All through the 1920s and 1930s the major European powers continued to supervise their colonies. In several places, with the Italians in Eritrea for example, and the French in Morocco, the lines were originally laid down specifically for military purposes and later adapted to civilian use.

The first French lines in Morocco were particularly interesting since they were somewhat similar in concept to the Austrian railways in Bosnia. The Algeciras affair of 1911-12 meant that standard-gauge lines were, at least for the time being, forbidden but the French lost no time in building instead a strategic network on the 60cm gauge. Especially towards the Algerian frontier the gradients and curves were very severe and it proved necessary to provide locomotives of considerable power. The lines were converted to standard gauge after

World War 1 and the stock was dispersed.

25 Decauville 0-6-0+0-6-0 for Morocco

Most powerful and ingenious of the 60cm gauge machines was a series of articulated tender locomotives built from 1912 onwards. These were Mallet simples, having four identical high-pressure cylinders and with steam connections by flexible pipes instead of the more usual ball joints. Their major interest lay in the fact that, for reasons of standardisation, they had many parts in common with the standard DV 0-6-0Ts of the French army. In particular the forward bogie was a complete 0-6-0 chassis while the rear 'engine' used the same parts but had outside frames. A Belpaire firebox was fitted and the locomotives were equipped with the Soulerain vacuum brake. Leading dimensions were: length overall 11·32m; total wheelbase (loco) 4·1m; rigid wheelbase 1·40m; wheel diameter 0·55m; cylinders 215 by 280mm. As well as the locomotives a variety of bogie vehicles was built for the strategic lines. They were naturally of high capacity and were more substantially built than their artillery railway equivalents in metropolitan France.

THE RISE OF LONGMOOR

One positive result of the military railway interest generated by World War 1 was that almost all the contenders—at least the victorious ones—retained a base or bases for their railway troops. Railways had proved vital in that war; they might well, or so the theorists guessed, be equally useful in the next (especially if it was fought on similar lines as military thinking believed it would be!). At the same time World War 1 was the 'war to end war' and it had only just finished. Little money was therefore available for military development of any kind and transport had a very low priority. The result was that the military railway organisations had to exist on whatever they could collect while training their troops with an eye to the future.

Typical of such organisations was the British Army's main base at Longmoor in Hampshire. Originating as the Woolmer Instructional Railway—which clearly indicated its purpose—it had during World War 1 developed into a comprehensive network joining Liss on a main line to a standard-gauge branch at Bordon. Most of the railway troops used in France and other sectors received their initial training at Longmoor camp or at Bordon.

Longmoor, more than any other establishment, kept British military railways alive in the 1920s and 1930s, and it shared in the big revival of work during World War 2. Indeed it was only closed as a training railway in 1970, when the reduced role of railways in military transport had become self-evident. Most railway enthusiasts of today—and many military railway men—will remember it in its prime, with its stud of standard tender locomotives and 0-6-0STs, its occasional diesels and its neat blue-painted trains of ex-civilian coaches. Perhaps it is more of a tribute, then, to illustrate it by a little of the more motley stock that sustained the line in its uncertain days.

26 0-6-2T Thisbe

From the very beginning, Longmoor had a pleasant habit of giving its locomotives names. Thisbe was acquired second-hand by the Woolmer Instructional Railway in 1914, but was a comparatively new machine and typifies the 'short-stay' locomotives; W.D. equipment was freely transferred between depots and Thisbe, as W.D. 84, left for Rhyl (Kinmel Park) before 1918. Built by Hawthorn Leslie in 1911 for the Shropshire and Montgomeryshire Light Railway, she proved too heavy for that line, hence her sale. Dimensions were weight in WO: 36t; driving wheel diameter: 3ft 6in.; cylinders: 14in. by 22in.

27 L.M.R. breakdown crane

Just as a reminder that locomotives are not the 'be-all-and-end-all' of military railways, Longmoor did own a comprehensive collection of rolling-stock. One of their prides for many years was this massive Ransomes and Rapier steam crane, complete with matchwagon. On a military training railway such devices were even more necessary than on civilian lines!

THE PATHOS OF WAR

28 Farewell—1

Inevitably war has many bitter and poignant moments and railways, as a major transport service, saw their fair share of these. Most of the fighting men on both sides at some time in their service careers were seen off at their local railway station or a big city terminus—and considerably fewer returned through the same portals. If this little cameo provides even a glimpse of the way in which all man's technological advances can be used to destructive ends it may serve its purpose.

29 Farewell—2

Besides troops, the railways both in Britain and on the Continent carried people to save their lives—refugees and evacuees by the tens of thousands. One of the most organised exoduses of this kind in the early part of the war was the precautionary evacuation from England's big cities of thousands of children 'billeted out' on country families. The major London termini in particular saw many touching scenes of this sort.

IMPROVISED ARMOURED TRAINS

30 SG armoured train (G.B.)

In the Boer War, armoured trains had been used to control long lines of communication, and ever since then they had been thought of as possibly useful for such purposes. Their first serious application in World War 2 was quite different. In June 1940 the British Army had been driven off the continent of Europe, losing most of its mobile equipment and heavy weapons in the process. In spite of much barrel-scraping in the armament depots and some requisitioning of civilian vehicles, the army was very badly equipped, and invasion was expected almost hourly. In consequence, all along the south coast in particular, use was made of railways where these could form part of a defence system. The Southern Railway in particular had a number of lines running more or less parallel to the coast and thus providing lateral communication links. What could be more natural than to try to use them also to provide desperately needed mobile fire power. In consequence the main-line companies' works turned out, for the military, improvised armoured trains like that shown here. This one operated around Wadebridge in Devon and consisted of a former L.N.E.R. branch line 2-4-2T, running push-pull between four four-wheeled wagons; two wagons next to the engine carried supplies and the outer ones were provided with guns. Although the whole train was camouflaged, it is interesting to note that only the gun wagons had any armour; the motive-power unit was virtually unprotected and would not have lasted long in action. Fortunately the invasion never materialised.

31 Detail of gun-wagon (G.B.)

The gun-trucks of the Wadebridge train were normal 10–12 tonne open chassis clad in a bodywork of concrete and mild steel—which, while not ideal, was all that was available. The accommodation was in two parts. At the outer end was a compartment mounting a small ex-naval gun—probably a two-pounder—and cut away to provide a 180° arc of fire. Behind it was a high-walled 'command bunker' containing the truck commander and several infantrymen who were provided with slots through which to fire small arms. The underframe was not protected in any way.

32 Narrow-gauge gun-wagon (G.B.)

An interesting, if on the face of it somewhat ludicrous, variation on the armoured train appeared in Kent during June/July 1940. Here the very narrow-gauge (15in.) Romney Hythe and Dymchurch Railway ran in a sweeping arc along the eastern side of the Dungeness peninsular. That area with its excellent beaches was certain to be a prime target for any invasion and the unit defending it decided to make use of the railway as a lateral communication link. To provide mobile firepower it, too, acquired an armoured train.

Like its bigger brother the train consisted of a locomotive sandwiched between gun-wagons and its steel and concrete armouring was done at a Southern Railway works but there the resemblance ended. The R, H and D armoured train consisted of one of the line's 4-8-2 mixed traffic locomotives partly protected by steel plating and coupled between two bogie hopper wagons. These metal-bodied wagons had high sides already and were comparatively simple to armour. Each carried two Lewis guns and a Boys anti-tank rifle, at that time the only infantry anti-tank weapon available. The train was for a time kept constantly available and had steam up twenty-four hours a day. It was even provided with a camouflaged hide-out in the shape of an artificial tunnel erected near a disused station. Fortunately the invasion did not come but the unit did see service protecting troop movements in its anti-aircraft role and its crew have always claimed the destruction of at least one aircraft.

RAIL-BORNE ARTILLERY

33 British 9·2in. rail-mounted gun for cross-Channel bombardment

As in World War 1, both sides made limited uses of rail-mounted artillery—most of it, in fact, was if not the self-same weapons at least their very close brothers! The Germans probably made most use of rail-mounted heavy guns, both as mobile weapons on the Russian front and as part of their anti-invasion defences where some used the old trick of hiding in tunnels when they were not firing. There was, however, one extension of their use by both sides; in the Dover Straits the opposing forces were separated only by twenty miles or so of choppy water and each made arrangements for bombarding the other's coastal areas and for interfering in a desultory manner with coastal shipping. The German weapons lived in various hide-outs along the Cap Gris Nez area; the British had various sites including a whole complex of spurs springing from a junction with the Southern Railway in the St Margaret's Bay area. It utilised various works of a never-completed scheme—the St Margaret's Mill and Dover light railways—and ended in several gun positions behind the Dover cliffs. Heavy guns such as ex-World War 1 9·2in. mounting shown, were kept in concealment under camouflage-netting in various cuttings and were thence laboriously trundled into firing position when needed, by pairs of elderly 0-6-0s. Rather than provide permanent and easily visible recoil pits at the gun positions, it appears that a fairly complex 'lash-up' was used to absorb recoil. As can be seen from the picture this involved a series of steel hawsers anchored to bolts set in concrete and secured by massive turnbuckles. The latter would allow both adjustment of tension in the cables and a convenient and fairly rapid method of disconnecting the gun-wagon when it had to be moved.

GERMAN STANDARD WAR LOCOMOTIVES, 1939–45

As with their Prussian forebears, the German standard locomotive designs of the inter-war years showed a curious tendency to fit other people's loading gauges. No doubt desire for possible exports would account for much of this but none the less for such a peace-wishing country there were a number of peculiar features. For instance, once again all the heavy goods locomotives had their funnels in two parts for quick unbolting . . .

Any aspirations there might have been were certainly helped by the very high quality of design work. The new Reichsbahn in 1924 wanted strong, efficient machines and their design staff was able to start from scratch—interim orders could well be made up from the well-tried Prussian designs of which large quantities were already in service. In consequence a restricted number of standard designs was conceived to cover all the major requirements and particular attention was paid to ruggedness and ease of maintenance. Careful comparative studies were made of such things as the relative advantages of two- and three-cylinder designs, small numbers of otherwise identical locomotives being built as parallel classes for testing before final decisions were made. As a result the final designs were excellent and, whatever the intention, the goods locomotives in particular were well suited to war purposes. Nevertheless, as the war progressed even these were further simplified for production purposes, to such effect that over 6,000 of one type were produced between 1943 and the end of the war.

34 Class 44—2-10-0

Mainstay of the heavy goods programme in the original standardisation scheme was the Class 44 three-cylinder 2-10-0. An excellent machine in all respects it was quite capable of handling very heavy traffic and was used in considerable numbers during the 1930s. Leading dimensions were: overall length 22·62m; coupled wheelbase 6·80m; coupled wheel diameter 1·40m; cylinders 550 × 660mm; all-up weight 110·1t + 73·2t; maximum axle-load 19·8t.

35 Class 50—2-10-0

Introduced in 1939, this two-cylinder machine is probably the most famous goods locomotive produced in Germany. Officially classed as a 'light' locomotive it was deliberately designed with a low axle-loading for use over secondary routes where the 44s would have been too powerful. 1,200 were already on order in 1939 and the design was both simple, and rugged. It was very soon simplified even further, along with the 44 class, as the so-called 'U.K.' or 'Bergangs-Kriegslokomotive (Transitional War Locomotive). Leading dimensions were: overall length 22·94m; coupled wheelbase 6·60m; coupled wheel diameter 1·40m; cylinders 600 × 660mm; all-up weight 86·8t + 60t; maximum axle-load 15·2t.

36 Class 52—2-10-0

The urgent demand for motive power led, in 1942, to the decision to further simplify various classes and to give locomotive production high priority. The 'new' machines were to be based firmly on existing designs but were to be stripped of any inessential fittings and were to be weatherproofed to stand up to the extreme conditions experienced on the Russian front.

The first class to be unveiled, in September 1942, was a variant of the ubiquitous '50'. This was the obvious choice since with its light axle-loading it could operate over the somewhat rickety tracks in the East.

Simplification was ruthlessly carried out, to the extent that it was possible to eliminate about one-fifth of the individual parts required to build a '50' and to simplify over half of the remainder. The resulting locomotive had smaller running-boards, no smoke deflectors or feedwater heaters while the original bar-frames were replaced by plate-frames—slightly less strong but easier to produce. The main connecting rods were welded from three pieces instead of being expensively machined from the solid and the Walschaerts valve gear was effectively simplified. The cabs were fully enclosed to cope with the Russian winter and contained the more delicate equipment such as the steam valves and injectors; the air brake pumps for the Knorr brakes were lagged with glass wool fibre. Originally, straight-sided eight-wheeled tenders were fitted but later locomotives had semi-vanderbilts, frameless bogie tenders. Experiments were made with various trial features such as welded boiler barrels and frames to try and simplify production still further but none were adopted as standard. Almost 7,000 Class 52s were built between 1942 and 1945, many being supplied to German allies such as Bulgaria, Romania and Hungary. They were used all over the occupied countries and after the war some 3,500 were expropriated by the victors as reparations. Most of these have been used in the communist countries, in particular Poland (over 1,100 units) and Russia; the Russian ones have, of course, been re-gauged. In western Europe only Austria retained 52s in quantity into 1973, their 152 class being the bar-framed variety.

Leading dimensions of the 52 (with semi-vanderbilt tender) were: overall length 22·975m; coupled wheelbase 6·50m; coupled wheel diameter 1·40m; cylinders 600 × 660mm; all-up weight 84t + 60t (tender); maximum axle-load 15t.

37 Class 42—2-10-0

The 52 proved so successful, despite a few design faults, that a simplified version of the heavy Class 44 was also produced from mid-1943 on, under the designation Class 42. In the light of experience with the 52s, slightly less simplification was attempted. Thus the running-boards were reduced but smoke deflectors could be fitted; no feedwater heaters were provided but the original pattern of bar-frames was largely adopted instead of plate-frames. Like the 52, the 42s had fully enclosed cabs but most of the 3,000-odd produced were employed within German frontiers and on main lines where their 18-tonne axle-load was not a handicap. The specification required that they be able to haul 1,600 tonnes at 60km/h on level track and, within their limitations, they were quite successful. Leading dimensions were (with semi-vanderbilt tender): overall length 23·00m; coupled wheelbase 6·60m; coupled wheel diameter 1·40m; cylinders 630 × 660mm; all-up weight 96·5t + 60t; maximum axle-load 17t.

38 Class 52 Condensing Locomotive

The vast, and at times arid, plains of Russia brought plenty of problems to the German railway troops. One attempt to conserve precious water was the use of condensing tenders, as fitted here to a 52 class 2-10-0. Ironically they did not come into service until the Germans were well on the retreat but 141 were built before the war's end and a few more were completed afterwards.

CIVILIAN LOCOMOTIVES AT WAR

39 Reichsbahn Class 03[10] 4-6-2

Typical of the 'prestige' locomotives in all countries that had to be pressed into more mundane duties during the war were the sixty streamlined German light pacifics of Reichsbahn class 03[10]. Some of the most handsome express locomotives ever built, they put in a great deal of hard work during the war and only forty-five of the class survived it. Leading dimensions were: length overall 29·9m; coupled wheel diameter 2·00m;

maximum axle-load 18·4t; cylinders 470 × 660mm.

40 Reichsbahn Class 94¹ 0-10-0T

No greater contrast can be imagined than the heavy shunting locomotives which in all countries performed much unsung work pushing war materials around the marshalling yards. Typical were the German tanks of Class 94 represented here not by the usual Prussian version but by the lesser known variant of the Württemberg State Railways. The class was originally built for light railway work, having a maximum axle-load of only 13 tonnes, but by the war years was on heavy shunting duties. The last survivor did not disappear until 1961. Leading dimensions were: length 11·03m; wheel diameter 1·15m; cylinders 500 × 560mm.

BIRDS OF A FEATHER

41 U.S. Army 2-8-0

As in World War 1, the United States Army settled for a rugged, simple, two-cylinder 2-8-0 as its standard freight locomotive. No doubt the transport authorities would have ideally preferred something more massive and powerful—there were plenty of examples on U.S. railways—but as before they had to consider where the locomotives might run. European railroads were known to be comparatively spindly affairs with restricted loading gauges and short turntables; most of the railways in the Middle and Far East hardly bore thinking of! The design therefore emerged as a simple development of the earlier design, a sturdy 130-tonner with a maximum axle-load of 15¾ tonne and a sustained tractive effort of 31,500lb. Length was 61ft 0¼in., coupled wheelbase 15ft 6in. and the coupled wheel diameter was 4ft 9in. Provision was made for either coal or oil firing and to suit various conditions both air and vacuum brakes were fitted for train operation. The locomotive itself had steam brakes in the normal American tradition.

42 Russian Army 2-8-0

Virtually identical with the U.S. Army locos—and with good reason—were 200 2-8-0 freight locomotives built by Baldwin and ALCO in 1943. They were, indeed, originally intended for the U.S. Army but were re-gauged and diverted to Russia under the Lease-Lend programme. The Russians classed them Wᵃ (the little 'a' indicating American) and soon fitted them with more commodious enclosed cabs as their climatic conditions required. Although by West European standards these are fairly big freight locomotives, in Russian eyes they are relatively puny and were soon relegated to light work. Many survived well into the 1960s.

RUSSIAN LOCOMOTIVES

43 Class B(5) 4-6-0

Particularly during the early part of the war, before American Lease-Lend supplies became significant, the Russian railways were hard-pressed. German attacks caused considerable casualties among locomotive stock and many older designs had to be used for military purposes. Prominent among these was the old B class 4-6-0 designed at the former Imperial Railways Briansk Works and built between 1908 and 1913 to a total of about 250. Many had been sold out of service between the wars to the Baltic States, in particular Latvia, and were there for the taking when these states were reoccupied in 1940! The Class B (transliteration from the Cyrillic 5) had an all-up weight, less tender, of 74·5 tonnes, a maximum axle-load of only 15·7 tonnes and six-foot coupled wheels.

44 Class S (Cyrillic C) 2-6-2

Backbone of most of the lighter work throughout the war was the S-class 2-6-2 designed in 1910 at Sormovo works. With a total of over 3,000 built, the class might almost be called the Russian P8 and it was certainly nearly as ubiquitous; like the P8, there were constant improvements during the long production run, which only ended in 1951. Typical dimensions of a 'mid-batch' locomotive included a locomotive weight of 84 tonnes, a maximum axle-load of 18 tonnes and coupled wheels 6ft 0¾in. in diameter.

45 Class Ye (E) 2-10-0

The main locomotive type supplied by America under the Lease-Lend agreements was a heavy 2-10-0 by Baldwin and ALCO, some 2,120 in all being produced. As with the standard U.S. Army 2-8-0, this was a straightforward 'repeat' of a design that had also been supplied to Russia during World War 1; it would seem that the rugged simplicity and ease of production of these locomotives outweighed any subsequent advances in locomotive design! It is recorded that as Russia was not officially at war with Japan, the machines were shipped direct from the U.S. to Vladivostock using Russian ships. Leading dimensions were: all-up weight (engine) 90t, maximum axle-load 16·2t, coupled wheel diameter 4ft 4in.

FLOTSAM AND JETSAM—CIVILIAN LOCOMOTIVES IN WAR USE

As usual (or is this too cynical?) the British Army at the outbreak of World War 2 found itself very ill-equipped in the military transport sphere. The motley collection of second-hand machines that provided rail motive power for the various depots—in particular for Longmoor—were by no means sufficient for the traffic that was likely to develop. For home and shunting use a number of light tank engines was acquired in small numbers from various railway companies; the W.D. seemed especially fond of ex-Great Eastern 0-6-0Ts.

46 Dean Goods 0-6-0

Mainstay of the hastily assembled W.D. fleet, however, were the old faithfuls—ex-ROD 2-8-0s of World War 1 vintage and the ever-dependable Dean Goods 0-6-0s shown here. The Great Western Railway might consider these veterans distinctly superannuated and were no doubt quite pleased to find a buyer for them; the War Department knew from past experience in World War 1 that they were reliable, tough machines with a light enough axle-load to go almost anywhere they might be wanted. Accordingly they once more acquired over 100 of the class and shipped them hither and thither. France, Africa, India, the British Isles (where some rather oddly got fitted with pannier tanks); where the war was there also were the Dean Goods.

47 Bulleid Q1 Class 0-6-0

Not a military machine but symptomatic of the effect of war on civilian railways was the Bulleid 0-6-0 goods locomotive for the Southern Railway. Based on the existing Q class goods engine it typified the austerity regime of war which tried to save precious ferrous metals wherever possible. Hence the Q1—and its multifarious cousins in countries which included even massive Duplexii—dispensed with such frills as running plates used non-essential materials wherever possible and, inevitably, looked hideously ugly to railwaymen accustomed to traditional lines. Admittedly the Q1 was a rather extreme example . . .

W.D. STANDARD LOCOMOTIVES

48 British War Department 0-6-0ST

The 'standard' shunting locomotive for the British Army was the so-called Austerity 0-6-0ST developed from an industrial design of the Hunslet Engine Co. It came on the scene comparatively late, W.D. requirements up to about 1942 being met by requisitioning civilian locomotives of various types. When, however, it became clear that the European mainland would have to be invaded, a standard machine was obviously going to be needed. In typical British fashion, the military looked round to see what existing designs could be adapted. The choice lay between the simple and rugged 'Jinty' 0-6-0T of the L.M.S. and the equally rugged '18 inch' Hunslet Industrial 0-6-0T. The latter was favoured because of its shorter wheelbase and greater simplicity, which made for route availability and ease of production. Some 378 were built by the war's end, the same design being produced by various manufacturers, and they were used on all the European fronts. As with other military designs they were scattered far and wide after 1945, serving civilian railways in places as far apart as Holland and Tunisia; survivors were still running in the 1970s. Oddly, too, after disposing of huge numbers, the W.D. later ordered another fourteen in 1952-3 for use at depots in this country. Basic dimensions are: all-up weight 48·2t; maximum axle-load 16·35t; coupled wheel diameter 4ft 3in.; coupled wheelbase 11ft; cylinders 18in. × 26in.

BRITISH STANDARD LOCOMOTIVES

49 'Austerity' 2-8-0 (G.B.)

Just as in World War 1, the British Army found itself largely unprepared in 1939 so far as provision of railway locomotives was concerned; just as in that war, it immediately looked around for a convenient civilian design that would fulfil its requirements with a minimum of modification. In 1916, it was Robinson's Great Central 2-8-0s that fitted the specification. In 1941 it was another 2-8-0, Sir William Stanier's 8F class freight locomotive for the L.M.S., that was chosen as the basis for a military machine. The Stanier 2-8-0 was already a fairly simple and rugged machine; it simply needed some modifications to facilitate mass production and a touch of austerity. Like other standard war locomotives it was produced by the thousand

and served in most theatres of war. Survivors left behind by the British Army or bought cheaply by badly knocked-about railways saw post-war service all over the world and were still soldiering on in remote places like Turkey in 1973. With an all-up weight of just under 126 tons, a tractive effort at 85% pressure of 34,215lb, a coupled wheelbase of 16ft 3in. and coupled wheel diameter of 4ft 8½in., it matched very closely its American equivalent and was an extremely versatile and useful machine. Overall length was 63ft 6in. and either coal- or oil-burning equipment could be fitted. The locomotive had a steam brake and was dual fitted for train operation.

50 **W.D. Standard 2-10-0**

For service on some overseas lines, even the moderate 15–16 ton axle-load of a 2-8-0 proved excessive, and a 2-10-0 version of the basic design was therefore built in some quantity. It was virtually identical to the 2-8-0 except for an increase in coupled wheelbase to 21ft, a length of 67ft 6in., and a maximum axle-load (on the tender) of 14 tonnes. All-up weight was just under 134 tonnes and the locomotive could of course be equipped for coal or oil firing; like the 2-8-0 it was dual-fitted for train operation but the locomotive brakes were Westinghouse air brakes. Oddly, two examples have been preserved, one at the Dutch Railway Museum at Utrecht (in W.D. livery) and one in Great Britain.

51 **W.D. 2-8-0 armoured version**

The damage that allied fighters were causing to enemy railway installations did not go unnoticed by allied railway authorities. The locomotives in particular were seen to be vulnerable to air attack and at least one standard Austerity 2-8-0 was experimentally fitted with armour. Boiler, cab and steam pipes were quite effectively protected but the problem of covering in wheels and motion proved more intractable. In the event it was not possible to find an effective compromise between protection and maintenance and the project was dropped. In any case British air superiority made it unnecessary.

WAR DEPARTMENT GARRATTS (BRITAIN)

Much less publicised than the standard Austerity locomotives was a series of big articulated machines built during the latter half of World War 2 for service overseas. Various strategic lines in British Colonies and Dominions were extremely short of motive power suitable for heavy haulage and the American 'MacArthur' 2-8-2, the 'standard' narrow-gauge war engine, was too small. Beyer Peacock therefore built some sixty-nine locomotives to the Garratt design, a system of articulation in which the cab and boiler unit is pivoted at its ends on massive power bogies; these in turn carry the water tank and fuel tender. Both heavy and light types were built, the heavy version being intended mainly for 3ft 6in. gauge lines in Africa. It was basically a 2-8-2+2-8-2 and in that form was supplied to the Gold Coast (now Ghana), to the Congo and to Rhodesia; a metre gauge 4-8-2+2-8-4 variant went to the Kenya–Uganda Railway.

The so-called light type, with a maximum axle-load of about 10 tonnes, was actually made up of two distinct designs: a 2-8-0+0-8-2 designed for Burmese Railways and developed into a 2-8-2+2-8-2; and a larger 4-8-2+2-8-4 developed from a pre-war design for Brazil. All metre-gauge machines, they were used mainly in India and Burma though a few went to East Africa. Note that all were ordered by the War Department and bore W.D. running numbers.

52 2-8-2+2-8-2 for Burma

This 'light' Garratt, built for the strategic lines in Burma in 1944, was a straight development of a standard Burma Railways design and had much in common with it. Fourteen were supplied, having 15½in. by 20in. cylinders, a weight in working order of just under 118 tonnes and a maximum axle-load of 10·5 tonnes. Only twelve reached their destination but all these survived the war and were taken into Burma Railways stock.

53 4-8-2+2-8-4 for Kenya

Final development of the heavy type was this variant, some seven of which were supplied in 1943 to the Kenya Railway (W.D. Nos 74418–24). Many parts were interchangeable with earlier versions and they were convertible to 3ft 6in. gauge. They had 19in. by 24in. cylinders, an all-up weight of 171·5 tonnes and a maximum axle-load of 13·25 tonnes.

MILITARY DIESELS, 1939–45

It is a little ironic that in World War 2, the military authorities made less use of internal-combustion engined locomotives than they did in World War 1. The reason lies almost entirely in the different natures of the two wars. World War 1 use was almost entirely on the static light railways which required large numbers of small tractors; in World War 2 few such lines were needed since the war was largely one of movement; at the same time petrol products were always in short supply for both sides so that it was an advantage to use coal-burning locomotives. That natural fuel was comparatively plentiful and stocks were not nearly so vulnerable to enemy attack! Nevertheless both sides did make limited use of diesel locomotives where conditions required—for shunting, for use around dumps and explosive works, in desert conditions where coal and water were in shorter supply than petrol at times. All three major participants in the western sector had standard designs, only Russia relying entirely on steam.

54 W.D. 0-6-0DE

The British War Department adopted its usual policy of looking for existing civilian designs suitable for its own requirements. Fortunately the London Midland and Scottish Railways had for some years previously been experimenting with diesel locomotives for shunting purposes and had evolved a standard six-coupled diesel-electric design. The W.D. simply acquired these in small numbers and used them, in conjunction with some American Lease-Lend equipment, where it thought necessary. They were not a significant factor in the British military railways although one somehow managed to end up on a French light railway, the CF de Mamers à St Calais, where it was still in occasional use in 1973. The plate shows one that was in post-war years sent to the Longmoor Military Railway. Horsepower was 350hp.

55 Wehrmacht 0-6-0DH

German equivalent of the L.M.S. design, but built in much greater numbers, was the 360-hp machine shown here. This 42 tonne 0-6-0 had Voith hydraulic drive via a jackshaft and was used extensively in shunting, movement of railborne artillery and in rear areas. More than 200 of them came into stock with the civilian Deutsche Bundesbahn alone after 1945 and many others found a home in other countries. Some were still in D.B. departmental use in 1973 while others were serving with various minor railways. Leading dimensions were: length 9·24m; wheelbase 4·40m; wheel diameter 1·10m.

56 Whitcomb B-B (U.S.A.)

The standard U.S. Army machine, produced with variations mainly by the American Locomotive Co., by Baldwin and by Whitcomb, was a much more substantial affair. Although by American standards it was only a yard shunter (switcher) it was a double-bogie design powered by two 325-hp motors and quite suitable for trip-working under European conditions. The type was produced in quantity for the Allied forces and was used in North Africa, in Italy and, after D-day, in north-west Europe. Some stayed in Europe after 1945, no less than ten being bought by one particular French minor railway while the Longmoor line acquired two

(W.D. 890/1). Drive was diesel-electric and the main dimensions were: length 42ft 9in.; bogie wheelbase 7ft; wheel diameter 3ft 3in.

MOVEMENTS BY RAIL

57 Build-up of locomotives

The movement of all these locomotives naturally resulted at times in what might almost be called traffic-jams, especially in the United Kingdom. In Germany new locomotives could be worked up to their operational areas in revenue-earning trains, for there was always material that needed moving. In England the build-up for the proposed invasion of Europe meant the construction—and import—of many more locomotives than were currently required. Hence there was a great deal of movement of 'trains' of locomotives to storage areas, and sights such as this were common. Here a W.D. Austerity 2-8-0 tows a collection of freshly imported U.S. Army locomotives of the same wheel arrangement.

58 Tank trucks into coal wagons

Up to about 1943, movements of heavy war material by rail in the United Kingdom was vulnerable to enemy air attack and various subterfuges were indulged in to try and camouflage valuable loads. British camouflage specialists were by this time very competent in designing wood and canvas mock-ups and so it was natural they should try to use them on railways. The plate shows the general way in which vehicles, mounted on standard bogie wagons, were concealed. Simple canvas 'dodgers' were erected round the wagon sides, painted to represent coal wagons, and the protruding turrets were covered with coal-flavoured camouflage netting.

59 Concealed tank on wagon

This close-up shows a typical wagon. It must be remembered that at that period private-owner wagons still existed in profusion despite pooling arrangements so that the sight of wagons with large names blazoned on them was fairly common. The subterfuge would not have deceived a close observer but against a rapidly moving aircraft it had a reasonable chance.

OVERSEAS CAMPAIGNS—THE MIDDLE EAST

Quite apart from their massive use on the 'home fronts' railways were of course used by the military authorities of both sides in the various Middle East campaigns which waxed and waned during 1941-5. Most were civilian lines taken over or partly controlled by the military and they did perform a useful if not vital role in supplying the fighting men.

60 El Alamein

If everyone thinks of the North African campaigns as largely motorised ones they are not entirely right. Besides the rear-area railways, in Tunisia for the Axis and in Egypt for the British, the military did run single feeder lines along the coast towards their forward positions. The Axis used a certain amount of 95cm gauge centred on Benghazi, the British had a W.D.-worked standard-gauge line extending up to and past the Alamein positions. It was worked by a miscellaneous collection of W.D. and Egyptian State Railways stock.

61 Eritrea

Much less famous than the Alamein campaign were the earlier battles against the Italians for the colonies of Eritrea and Somaliland. That part of Africa had been colonised by various European powers around the turn of the century and the Italians were prominent among them. The country was rugged and the conquerors early on built an impressive narrow-gauge railway to join their main port of Massawa to the interior. Military use of the line reached its peak in the 1920s and 1930s. Then Mussolini's dreams of a grand Italian Empire led to a determination to conquer the neighbouring country of Ethiopia. Asmara was the jumping-off point and the railway was used to bring up supplies in conjunction with an aerial ropeway— a situation reminiscent of the Austro-Italian campaign in World War 1. Possession of the main transport artery did not however save the Italians from defeat in 1941.

THE ITALIAN CAMPAIGN

62 First train Naples-Rome

The first allied foothold on the mainland of western Europe was in Italy— consequential on the successful invasion in 1943. The Italian railways at that period must be considered as perhaps the least fortunate of all the major European systems. Even before the official capitulation of Italy, its transport systems were in fact strictly controlled by its German allies who had no illusions about the need for close supervision;

they certainly did not trust the civilian staff. After the capitulation the railways in the German held areas were even more firmly controlled. The others were in chaos, first because the Allied airforces bombed and strafed mercilessly to hamper German communications, and secondly because the Germans themselves made a thorough job of destroying lines as they withdrew. In consequence the military railway engineers came very much into their own. The railways had, of necessity, to come under direct military control and the railway troops found themselves doing major reconstruction work and a good deal of operating as well. Large quantities of standard U.S. Army and W.D. equipment were used to supplement the surviving Italian stock and this plate shows a typical scene during the restoration of services. At Roccasecca, close to the notorious Highway 6, troops of 150 Construction Company RE have just finished restoring the badly damaged track. The first train towards Rome, symbolically hauling Engineers' mechanical equipment, is powered by two of the U.S. Whitcomb BB diesels of 650 hp (Pl. 59), supplied under Lease-Lend and very useful when water supplies were, to say the least of it, uncertain.

IMPROVISED ARMOUR AGAIN

63/4 Russian armoured trains

The British were not the only combatants in World War 2 to improvise armoured trains in a rather hasty fashion. The Russians entered the war involuntarily in 1941 as a result of a massive German attack and were soon retreating rapidly before the Panzer columns. Both sides found the vast distances a great handicap since it was almost impossible to maintain a proper front line, and the Russians were initially very short of transport and of mobile fire power.

In this situation the Russian propaganda worked wonders, creating a team spirit among production workers that resulted in considerable feats; in more than one beleagured city, tanks and other vehicles were constantly being completed and delivered to the defenders even while the siege was in progress. The same spirit obviously animated a group of workers, who, in their own time, produced an armoured train as 'a present for the Red Army'. The massively boxed-in locomotive appears to be a variant of the o-class 0-8-0 or possibly an 0-10-0; the box shapes contain the dome with its adjacent regulator casing and an odd cylindrical tank, which was mounted above the rear portion of the boiler on some locomotives. The two major gun trucks, mounting one quick-firing field gun apiece, are noteworthy both for their design—a simple armoured hut —and for the fact that the whole superstructure is mounted on a turntable, thus giving the gun a very wide field of fire at the expense of some vulnerability.

65/6 Armoured wagons

These two plates show variations on a theme of how to armour an ordinary steel goods wagon with minimum alteration. In each case the full wagon structure has been retained, entry being via the original doors, but has been given additional armour plate and has had an armoured roof erected on it; it is interesting to compare Pl. 66, the wagon arranged for infantry occupation, with the very similar bogie wagon produced during the Boer War (Vol. I, Pl. 15). Indeed the Russian campaign brought together two features of earlier armoured trains; there was a desperate need for mobile firepower, however cumbersome, and there were very long lines of communication to contend with. One can even, in some ways, compare the roving mechanised columns with the mobile Boer commandos of 1899! It is therefore not surprising that armoured trains were once again in use.

ARMOURED VEHICLES AGAIN

67 Sd Kfz 231 on rails

The vast distances covered in Russia in particular also led the Germans to try and protect their supply routes with armoured vehicles. Unlike the Russians, they felt that armoured trains were rather cumbersome and so tended to use smaller units. Fortunately (or foresightedly) their standard eight-wheeled armoured car the Sd Kfz 231 (8-rad) series had been specially designed so that with minimum modification it could be adapted to rail use. Along with a batch of captured French Panhards, a number was used to patrol vulnerable lines.

68 Czech armoured trolley

Another vehicle used for patrolling such lines was an updated version of the armoured trolley illustrated in *Railways and War before 1918*. Apart from a general 'smoothing off' of the angles, no doubt to allow for the improved ballistics of modern weapons, it was surprisingly similar to its predecessor. It was of course a pure rail vehicle and not convertible.

EFFECTS OF ALLIED BOMBING

69 The bombing of Bielefeld

If railways were essential communication links in Russia, in western Europe they were just as vital. One of the major lessons learnt in World War 1 was the way in which rail communications were vulnerable to air strikes. One of the lessons not really learnt until after the war had ended was that direct bombing was not, perhaps, the best way of destroying a railway; it was surprisingly easy, outside major stations and yards, to minimise the effects and repair damage quickly. As an example one can take the Infuriating Matter of the Bielefeld Viaduct. This north German bridge lay on a vital link between the northern ports and the industrial Ruhr. For four years, British and American heavy bombers pounded it, covering the ground for hundreds of yards with near misses. Finally, in early 1945, a 10-ton 'earthquake' bomb dropped close alongside, undermined the piers and the viaduct collapsed. 'No more trains will pass over this line' said a triumphant newsreel commentator of the period as the awesome sight was revealed. . . . Unfortunately what was not visible was the beautifully camouflaged double-track diversion that had been waiting for just that day. From a concealed junction south of the viaduct it swung down into and up out of the river valley in a wide sprawling loop that must have enabled traffic to operate with very little break at all. Indeed it was in use for some years after the war until full working over the viaduct was restored. Plain track, and even many engineering works rarely justified the weight of bombs spent on them and the Germans were adept in camouflaging repairs so that destruction still seemed complete.

STRAFING AN EMMETT

70 'Strafing an Emmett'

As the Allies became stronger, in 1941-2, they began offensive intruder operations over occupied Europe to supplement the bombing campaign. Flights or squadrons of heavily armed fighters would roam around over France and the Low Countries with the expressed intentions of shooting up anything that moved—thereby hoping to disrupt the enemy's communications. The idea was quite realistic, four 20-mm cannon being quite powerful enough to allow one aircraft to wreak havoc on a train or road convoy, and much damage was undoubtedly done. Yet there was one more poignant aspect highlighted by the occasional casual report of pilots that they had 'shot up an Emmett' (i.e. a quaint-looking train). Almost invariably this meant that the target was one of the little 'tortillards' or local railways that were almost the only form of mechanical transport left to the country villagers. The pilots could not be blamed for not knowing; a train was a train was a train, and with the very short time lapse between spotting a moving vehicle and rushing past it, they usually shot on sight. For the local communities, however, the event could well be a disaster. As the main form of transport the train could well be packed so that some casualties were likely; even if no one was killed valuable livestock might well suffer. More important, the railway company was probably impecunious to start with, and had little stock to spare even in normal circumstances. In wartime, with its railcars immobilised for want of fuel, and with arrears of maintenance mounting steadily, a shot-up locomotive and stock might well mean no train the following day. The plate shows just such a scene on the rather run-down system of the Chemin de Fer de Flandres up in the north-east of the country. The train has come to a grinding halt at the first sign of attack. The elderly Corpet Louvet metre gauge 0-6-2T has been hit sufficiently to wreath it in steam—not a difficult matter since even one 20-mm round piercing the boiler shell would suffice. The vehicles are already riddled and the passengers have prudently taken cover wherever possible with such of their belongings as they can grab. In this case it is not the enemy who suffers but the inhabitants of the occupied territory.

LIGHT RAILWAYS AT WAR

71 Smuggling

When they were working, light railways in the German-occupied zones of Europe occasionally found themselves actively involved in the war at home—the constant battle between occupying troops and the local resistance groups. Up till November 1942, for example, France was divided into occupied and unoccupied zones. Several light railways ran across the borders and it was not unknown for them to participate in smuggling weapons and other small objects. An oilskin-wrapped package in the water tank or under the coal stood a good chance of escaping detection. Perhaps one might mention here that the light railways sometimes got involved in ways more frustrating to themselves. There was, for instance, the metre-gauge line of the CF du Dauphiné, in the French Alps, that found itself with one end controlled by the Germans, the other by the local maquis; not only were trains constantly being halted for inspection by both sides but passengers had to provide themselves with two appropriate sets of papers... not very conducive to traffic. A sister line in the same area was even more unfortunate; having against its will to transport German troops it suddenly found itself almost denuded of motive power when the maquis blew up its main depot. Even more infuriatingly for the railway, its sole surviving locomotive was similarly treated when it returned home the following night.

72 Revival in the Channel Isles

Oddly, the war did occasionally lead to the building of new light railways where none had been before or where former trackbeds were available. One such area was the Channel Isles, the only part of British territory actually occupied by the Germans during World War 2. On two of these islands, Jersey and Guernsey, there had been civilian light railways but the lines had been closed prior to the war. It was therefore with some surprise that the inhabitants observed their 'liberators' briskly proceeding to build quite extensive networks, using material acquired from various mainland sources. Metre, 90cm and 60cm gauges were all employed. The main purpose of the lines was to help construct and service the coastal defences that became part of the vaunted 'West Wall' but the Germans also made quite an event of the 'opening' in Jersey with a decorated locomotive and a small ceremony. The promise was that a new era of transport was dawning, but in practice the lines were comparatively little used after completion of the defences and those remaining were quickly removed by the islanders after liberation as part of their attempts to wipe out all memory of the occupation.

73 Heeresfeldbahn 0-8-0

As in World War 1, the Germans made some use of military field railways and produced standard six-, eight- and ten-coupled locomotive designs for use on them. Unlike the previous war lines, most of these field railways were of 75cm gauge, a measurement that also allowed the Germans to utilise the major narrow-gauge systems in Poland and at various other places along the Russian front. Many such locomotives were taken over by others after the war for civilian use. Notable were a big batch of 0-8-0s by Franco Belge, built in 1944-5. Most of these ended up as tank locomotives, either in France on sugar-beet lines or in Austria on various narrow-gauge branches. Some became tender-tanks, ending up as the Austrian Federal Railways 699 Class. Here 699.03, for long the reserve locomotive on the Pinzgauerlokalbahn, is shown in öBB livery.

74 Gazelle

In Britain the War Department took over several ailing minor lines—usually

113

because they were remote and virtually devoid of traffic! One was the long and straggling Shropshire and Montgomeryshire Light Railway, running west from Shrewsbury, which blossomed forth into a positive network of lines serving dumps and camps. Its locomotive stock was even more eccentric than the usual motley W.D. collection and soon discreetly vanished but the oddest one did get a fresh lease of life for some time. The little 0-4-2T Gazelle, perhaps the most curious standard-gauge locomotive in the country, was used as an inspection trolley for several years, patrolling the line each morning to check all was in order. She was preserved by the military after the war.

BUSES ON RAILS

75/6 Improvisation—1

In the occupied countries particularly, there was by 1942 a severe shortage of petrol for civilian road transport. The railways, especially local lines, found themselves with increased traffic and in some cases even closed branches were reopened. In at least one instance this was due to the enterprise of the local bus operator who had taken over the replacement bus services in 1938. This company realised that it could conserve precious tyres, etc., for other services by reinstating rail transport wherever road and rail ran parallel. In consequence two branches from Alencon, to Condé-s-Huisne and to Domfront, closed but not lifted, were put at its disposal. Standard Verney road buses of the period were quickly converted to rail use by substituting a fixed axle with flanged wheels for the former front axle and by replacing the twin rear wheels with flanged steel ones. The bus engines were converted to run on the wood-burning Imbert gas-producer system, the generators being mounted at the rear of each vehicle and fed by gravity from an ingenious box and chute installed on the former roof racks; the existing ladder access to these also gave convenient access to the generators. To avoid the problems of turning vehicles at each end of the line, they were coupled back to back in pairs, the leading bus only being under power at any one time.

It is recorded that the suspension and ride of these improvised railcars left much to be desired: every rail joint was distinctly felt, and with the poor maintenance of wartime there were plenty of defective joints! Nevertheless these buses gave good service from 1943 to 1946 and one pair, reconverted to petrol operation, were used on a local railway up to the 1960s.

77 Improvisation—2

Another ingenious attempt to relieve the shortage of road transport was the Talon road-rail system, also a French innovation. No photographic record survives of M. Talon's wartime vehicles; the plate shows a similar experiment in the south of France just after the war. The standard road bus was converted for rail travel quite simply. The front wheels were just raised off the ground and supported on a small platelayer's 'lorry' composed of two pairs of small wheels on axles joined by a cradle. At the rear a similar arrangement allowed the rear road wheels, complete with rubber tyres, to rest on the rails and thus provide traction and braking while the 'lorry' kept them on the lines. It was not unknown for the rail-bus to tow an ordinary coach or wagon though one shudders to think of the effect had there been a serious derailment. In any case, like most wartime improvisations, the idea did not survive less stringent conditions.

78 Improvisation—3

French light railways were not the only ones to find they had to improvise. The Belgian secondary network hurriedly resurrected a large number of their elderly steam locomotives and put gas producer units on some of their railcars. They also found themselves with a number of blown bridges and had to resort to quite complex measures to transfer stock to now isolated sections of track. A railcar is here being ferried rather precariously across the Meuse.

BUILD-UP TO INVASION, 1944

79/80 Railway loads

If the railways of occupied Europe were having a bad time of it, they were not the only ones. British lines were under pressure as well, if for slightly different reasons. The chains of depots served by such minor arteries as the Shropshire and Montgomeryshire Light Railway were only one symptom of a much greater concentration of military power; from 1942 onwards England in particular was being prepared as the springboard for an allied invasion of the European mainland. By the end of 1943 the whole country was in effect an arsenal, packed with men and equipment that would be needed when the great day came.

Inevitably, the military mind being what it is, these stocks of material were constantly being moved from place to place, being issued to units for training or being sent back to depots for repair. By late 1942 German air interference was sufficiently negligible for railways to be the obvious means of communication and long strings of flat cars loaded with various military stores were a common sight. All sorts of vehicles were pressed into use: new British and U.S.-built 'warflats', standard railway bogie wagons, even some of the old 'rectanks' surviving from the previous war. The plates show typical loads that were carried, their variety being caused mainly by two factors—length of the individual vehicle and its weight. The latter affected not only the number of vehicles on a wagon, because of the maximum permitted axle-load on certain stretches of track, but also the possible load combinations. It did not make for efficient haulage if one end of a wagon was groaning under a massive deadweight just below permitted load while the other bore a truck so light that the bogie springs were hardly compressed at all.

As a rule of thumb, the average bogie wagon could carry one armoured tracked vehicle, two small lorries or half-tracks, or up to three light trucks. In the latter case the limiting factor was usually length rather than weight. The Germans in their turn found that much the same rules applied.

TRANSPORTING LOADS BY ROAD AND RAIL

81 Rail by road

A sight common in these days of railway preservation but not so common in 1942 was the transport of rail vehicles by road where this was necessary. The idea was by no means new even in 1942; the German and Austrian railways in particular had for some years been using 'Strassenroller' or multi-wheeled transporters for carrying goods wagons to customers who had no industrial siding. Indeed they were often flippantly referred to as 'walking sidings'. The Allied vehicles were rather more improvised though no less effective. Here a standard U.S. Mack tank transporter and heavy tractor is being used to convey a 10-ton open-wagon. The vehicle was simply winched on and off the trailer like a tank, short lengths of rail being used to link the trailer deck with a siding track.

82 Road by rail

Much more common, of course, as already shown was the carriage of road vehicles by rail. When this was done in bulk-drive on/drive off facilities were sometimes provided but where single vehicles, or small quantities had to be moved, this was not always possible. In such cases it was normal to lift them bodily on to and off railway wagons by cranes. In this case a railway breakdown crane is being pressed into service to handle a DUKW—one of those strange but useful 2½-ton amphibious lorries that helped so much in landing early supplies during the invasion of Europe.

83 VIP load

An unusual load for British Railways during the invasion build-up period—and an interesting forerunner of the present civilian 'motorail' service—was the special train put at the disposal of General Montgomery. 'Monty' as the senior British commander, and the Commander-in-Chief's deputy, was constantly having to visit scattered units throughout the British Isles and at the same time had to keep in touch with General Headquarters and the War Cabinet. To ensure comparative comfort and speed a special train was therefore made up including modified vans with ramps and end-doors to carry his fleet of cars; he could thus get the best of both worlds, travelling by train to near his destination and then changing to an appropriate vehicle depending on who he was to visit. The plate shows an official Rolls—not a car usually associated with that particular General but one which was used on prestige occasions!

84 Enemy load problems

The Germans were also using their railways to the full for long-distance transport of military loads; indeed the increasing shortage of motor fuels made such a course inevitable. At the same time they were badly hampered by increasing Allied air activity which knocked out not only track but stock as well. The plate shows a fairly common result—a battered Pzkw IV tank being returned for repair on an equally battered four-wheeled wagon. Indeed the picture might well have been entitled 'If you don't get them the first time, get them the next', for the wagon has quite clearly already been the target of a bombing attack which has seriously distorted its frame; none the less shortage of stock frequently forced improvisations of this nature, vehicles having to run in a condition that no self-respecting civilian railway would dare to have allowed in normal circumstances.

CARRYING RAILWAY STOCK BY SHIP

Internal transfer of material before the invasion, however, was a comparatively minor matter for both sides as opposed to the problems posed by the invasion itself. The German post-invasion problems were really an intensification of their existing ones—bombing was heavier and disruption of the railway system by resistance fighters more frequent. The Allies were faced with two completely new situations: first they had to assume that little railway material would be left behind by a retreating enemy so that replacement track, locomotives and stock would be needed on a large scale; then they had to arrange to get such replacements over to the Continent with no certainty that adequate ferry terminals or port facilities would be available. Indeed it was almost certain that they would not be available, certainly in the early stages, yet as soon as a breakthrough was made railways would be vital to carry the vast tonnages of supplies required by mobile divisions. Elaborate preparations were therefore made.

85 Loading locomotives

Heaviest and most bulky objects were the big freight locomotives which would be required as early as possible. The one advantage was that these would be able to stay on the Continent once they got there so they could be sent over by specially fitted freighters. The plate shows an American 2-8-0 being landed on an improvised jetty using overhead block and tackle equipment. As in peacetime days, some ships were fitted with heavy handling equipment for this purpose since full harbour facilities could not be guaranteed.

86/7 Loading rail vehicles on to LSTs

Rolling-stock, however, unlike locomotives, had to be transferable back and forth across the Channel when needed. The process of transferring urgent supplies from rail to ship, in Britain, and from ship to lorry to rail in improvised harbours on the beach heads in France, was too cumbersome, took too much time and occupied too many men. Various ways were therefore adopted to allow cross-Channel ferry services using little more than 'hards' or concrete ramps leading to the water. Most of these required the use of standard or modified tank-landing ships and allowed for some variations in tidal levels. One of the problems was that tank-landing ships as opposed to the smaller tank-landing craft, drew a fair depth of water so could not conveniently beach themselves to take on cargo.

Tank-landing ships (landing ships, tank, or L.S.T. to give them their official names) were always in very short supply so it was clearly desirable to modify them as little as possible. If modification could be restricted to rails inset in the tank deck, for example, they could be dual purpose. Where the slope allowed therefore the system shown in these two plates was used. The line of rails sloped down past the water's edge, continuing for some distance under the sea. On them ran a built-up tilted trolley with rails on its upper surface. It was designed so that when the trolley ran down into the water its upper surface became horizontal, the rails on it joining the fixed-rail line on shore by hinged flaps. A standard L.S.T. could then open its bow doors and nose-in to the outer end of the ramp trolley so that rail wagons could—somewhat gingerly—be transferred directly into the hold. The trolley could be winched clear of the ramp to avoid damage by rough seas, and could be adjusted within fairly narrow limits according to the state of the tide on the other side, however, unloading was often direct on to the beach!

LOADING FERRY BOATS FROM AN IMPROVISED JETTY

In addition to the invaluable but scarce L.S.T.s, a number of purpose-built ferry boats was available since their normal cross-Channel runs had been abruptly terminated owing to hostilities! Since these had clear car or train decks they were obviously of potential use but they were designed to load from specialist loading jetties that would not be available on the French side. At least two were therefore modified for stern loading and unloading direct from open 'hards'. The plates show the process of docking and loading.

88 Approaching the 'hard'

Most boats were fitted for two or three lines of track. The shore rails therefore terminated at a vertical wall sited at such a height that it was about mid-tide level. The ship was modified to contain its own massively-built self-contained loading gantry in place of the original stern doors and was brought into the 'hard' stern first as in normal practice; it was then anchored a short distance offshore but in line with the rail tracks.

89 Lowering the gantry platform

In normal practice a hinged 'drawbridge' is attached to the shore jetty and raised or lowered by cranes to link with the ferry boat's stern. Since this could not be provided in France, it was replaced by a travelling gantry on the ship from which a drawbridge was suspended. This normally lay in place on the rear-end of the train deck but could be lifted clear and moved backwards until its inner end lined up with the ship's stern. It was then slowly winched down until the inner end could be linked direct to the ship's rails and the outer end could be lined up with the shore track.

90 Aligning the drawbridge

The shore end of the bridge was supported on four short legs which fitted on to an abutment and the whole thing was positively located in relation to the rail tracks by huge swivelling pins like those used to hold rail turntables in alignment; two can be seen in the raised position in the foreground of the picture, together with the slots into which they were lowered.

With the drawbridge secure, the pulleys were then unbolted from the drawbridge to which they were attached and were winched up clear of the rail-loading gauge.

91 Loading wagons

With the link complete, rail wagons could then be run directly on or off the ship; the drawbridge had a certain amount of play at each end, as in normal practice, to allow for variations in the state of the tide. When the wagons had been loaded or unloaded, the whole process was reversed; pulleys were attached, the drawbridge released and winched up and then moved back into the ship. There do not appear to have been any stern doors to close off the train deck so use in rough seas must have been limited—particularly in view of the considerable deadweight and rise in the centre of gravity occasioned by the big gantry structure.

ROAD/RAIL CONVERSIONS

92/3 Quarter-ton truck convertible for rail use

Another parallel to World War 1 was the way in which all participants in World War 2 produced road vehicles that could be converted for rail use. Besides the various armoured vehicles (Pls. 65–6) it was quite common for engineers to convert lorries permanently for permanent way work over lightly relaid tracks—there are Dodge and Bedford 15cwt trucks acting as industrial shunters in France to this day. A slightly more ambitious conversion in many ways was the 1939–45 equivalent of the Old Crewe Tractor. That had been an adaptation of the universal chassis of the period, the Ford Model T, for 60cm gauge use. This was a modification of the most common Allied light car of 1939–45, the Jeep, for standard-gauge purposes but the concept was very similar and the reasons behind it were the same. Basis was a standard Willys or Ford Jeep (General Purpose car). The vehicle already had four-wheel drive and a good range of gears so that the road wheels were simply made replaceable by flanged ones. Jack up the vehicle, change the wheels and away you went. Since the wheel hubs were identical it was also possible to provide simple stowage—two on the back where the spare wheel normally went and two inside the body, on the existing equipment bins over the rear wheel arches. The vehicle was used as an inspection runabout and for negotiation of rickety sections of track.

DESTRUCTION OF RAILWAYS

94/5 The hook

One of the axioms of war strategy is that if you have to retreat you should make the enemy's advance as difficult as possible. In particular you should destroy the lines of communication so far as you can, in order to hamper your enemy's build-up of supplies. In the early stages of World War 2 the battles moved too swiftly and unexpectedly for the defenders to do much in this line but later on it was a different story. The Axis forces gave ground only stubbornly and the Germans in particular were adept at doing the maximum damage if they had the time.

One of their more ingenious devices was 'the hook' or rail wrecker. This was essentially a beautifully simple concept— you just ripped the track up after you as you retreated. The device itself is basically a large down-pointing hook mounted on a flat wagon and provided with a coupling for attachment to a locomotive. The procedure was as follows: the hook, coupled to one or more heavy locomotives was positioned over the track and its point lowered into a hole dug between the sleepers. The rollers visible at the wagon rear were then adjusted to press lightly on the rail head and the whole cortège moved slowly off. The hook grabbed up the sleepers but at the same time the rollers prevented the rails from lifting; hence the sleepers, being the weaker element, were simply broken in half, thus making them completely useless. Some equipments were fitted additionally with chutes from which small-shaped explosive charges could be dropped on the rails and exploded to break them at intervals. Lay the odd booby-trap among the disturbed remains, and the advancing enemy had a considerable problem to deal with! These wagons were used fairly extensively during 1943-5, especially on the Russian and Italian fronts, and were very effective.

EISENBAHNTRANSPORT

96 Panzer-carrying train

The Allied invasion of France on 6 June 1944 caught the German defenders partly unprepared and also unclear about its significance. Was it the main invasion, as Field-Marshal Rommel believed, or was it merely a feint, as some of the General Staff thought. Previous events had led the Germans to believe the most threatened area was Pas de Calais and the mouth of the Seine. Consequently most of their armoured reserves, including some of the most powerful armoured divisions fielded by either side, were stationed well east of the Seine. By the time it became evident that Normandy was indeed the major invasion area, the Allies were well established; by the time, additionally, that Hitler had been persuaded to release the reserve divisions, the situation was critical. The armour was urgently needed, yet it had three or four hundred miles to travel and its commander had two major problems. Petrol supplies were very restricted—if the divisions drove to Normandy 'on their own tracks' they might well arrive with insufficient fuel to make a decisive attack. In addition travel by road was fraught with danger since prowling squadrons of fighter-bombers were always patrolling the rear areas by day and shooting up any transport columns they saw.

'Railway transport' was the answer said the planners, with visions of the efficient military railway organisation and its successes on the Russian and Balkan fronts. A comparatively small number of trains could take a whole division, it would be easy to supply concentrated anti-aircraft support—using the divisions own weapons if need be—and the vehicles would suffer little wear and tear. They were quite right about the anti-aircraft firepower; with vehicles firmly lashed to rail wagons, it was possible to use their anti-aircraft guns at all times and a Panzer division had a big collection of such weapons. What they forgot, or did not seriously consider, was the difficulty of working trains through hostile occupied country over which the enemy had almost complete air superiority. It was not necessary to attack the heavily defended trains. Judicious bombing of strategic bridges and junctions continually forced the Germans to divert their trains or halt them while repairs took place, and while a few trains could carry a whole division, they could also 'lock up' a whole division if they were stalled some distance from anywhere with unloading facilities. In addition the Resistance organisations were asked to make an all-out effort to disrupt the enemy's rail transport. It only needed an explosive charge under a rail to halt a train; another, exploded behind, would effectively strand it for a time. The accompanying bursts of fire from small groups were not much more than pin-pricks but they served the purpose of greatly irritating the German troops, and the Resistance groups could not be ignored; they had to be captured or driven off if that section of line was to be safe for following trains. Furthermore, although an armoured division is a highly effective force *en masse*, it is rather like using a sledgehammer to squash a fly if the division has to deal with a small mobile group of partisans in wooded country. There are many disadvantages! As a result, the German divisions spent days and even weeks making their way to the front line and even then arrived piecemeal and somewhat battered. The plate shows a typical hold-up, the train stalled by a strategic ambush and its protective troops beginning to try and clear the partisans from the adjoining wood.

97 Tank-carrying truck

Of course the German troops quickly learned some precautions. A most ingenious device was this ramp wagon that could be pushed ahead of the locomotive. Outwardly an ordinary wagon, it was provided with an end-loading ramp that could be lowered at any point on the track. Hence an armoured vehicle—usually an elderly infantry tank but occasionally one of the Division's own vehicles—could be carried in front of the train to give it a clear field of fire. If the train was held up by partisans, the ramp could be quickly lowered and the tracked vehicle simply driven off to give heavy support to infantry clearing the area of enemy troops. Its task finished, the tank could then reverse back up the ramp on to the wagon and resume its normal function.

98 Armoured truck

Another ingenious weapon, really a variant on the 'armoured train' idea, was this armoured truck. It was again intended to be pushed in front of the locomotive and consisted basically of a much strengthened four-wheeled wagon heavily protected against blast damage. A dual-purpose plough for clearing snow and debris was fitted to the front and on top was a steel superstructure supporting a standard tank turret, complete with gun and commander's cupola; in this case the turret is that of a Pzkpfw IV with the long 75-mm L48 gun. The use of a complete turret was the product of typical Teutonic ingenuity and similar devices were often adopted as fixed strongpoints in defence lines. They gave good protection to the crew and offered a smaller target than the usual casemate while the modern 75mm gun had just as much power as the obsolescent naval guns of larger calibre that were more usually used on armoured trains. This particular pattern of wagon was of use mainly when mobile enemy forces were likely to be encountered in some strength; it was not so well adapted to dealing with pin-prick attacks by small groups of lightly-armed partisans.

THE FAR EAST

99/100 Japanese armoured car on rails

Not to be outdone by the Allies and the Germans, the Japanese in the Far East also had convertible road/rail vehicles. For instance their 'standard' six-wheeled armoured car—of which comparatively few were produced—was specifically designed for such purposes. Unlike Allied designs which usually involved changing complete wheels, it featured dismountable wheel rims. These were in effect steel rail tyres which bolted on to the existing wheel rims when required and which were usually carried hung on the vehicle sides. A typical vehicle had four-wheel drive to the rear axles, weighed 7 tons and was powered by a six-cylinder 100bhp engine.

Mention of the Japanese armoured cars must bring to mind the Far East campaign. Railways played a comparatively minor part because of the nature of the country over which it was fought: for the most part it was jungle or islands. It did however produce the most notorious railway of the war, the infamous 'death railway'. Operationally this was a simple link between the Thai/Malaysian systems in the south and the Burmese railways in the north. The Japanese needed it to support their troops thrusting towards India and so they built it, with prisoner of war labour under what were—for Europeans at any rate—appalling conditions. Men died like flies under the harsh labour and broiling sun to complete a line that was of little value when it was finished; it is said a man died for every sleeper laid on its hundreds of miles of length. After the war the link was broken and only the truncated ends are now worked.

AFTERMATH

There is, inevitably, a certain amount of glamour and excitement attached to railways that are actually at war: the dramas of their work, the aerial attacks, the way in which they cope with conditions far removed from normal can be vividly portrayed. What people tend to forget is the continuing effect that war has on civilian railways once the actual fighting is over. Then they are vitally needed to help in the urgent task of rehabilitation, but at the same time they are probably most unlikely to be in a condition to do so. Those in the victor countries may well be largely intact, though exhausted by years of maximum effort and minimum maintenance; those in the landsthat have actually been fought over are likely to be physically greatly damaged and to be suffering from shortages of all kinds. Furthermore there is no longer the pressure from the former military authorities that did at least divert labour and materials into keeping them going!

World War 2 was the first—and, hopefully, the last—since the American Civil War to highlight the problems of such wholesale destruction. In World War 1 most of the railways outside a largely static battle zone were still functioning reasonably well at the end, and even in 1865, the 'normal' form of transport was still the horse. In 1945, rapid distribution and assistance depended largely on railways and motor road transport—and petrol was still very much in short supply. A very great strain, therefore, was thrown on the civilian railways of the occupied countries and particularly on those of Germany which had taken most punishment. It is much to their credit that they somehow managed to cope with the situation even though many improvisations had to be made at times.

Rolling-stock of any sort was in short supply but the shortage of serviceable passenger vehicles immediately after the war was desperate. At the same time, with the partitioning of occupied Europe between Russia and the West, there were vast numbers of refugees to be moved to places where they could be given help. 'Passenger' trains of open coal wagons hastily pressed into service were by no means uncommon sights, a grim prospect for their occupants in the autumn and winter of 1945.

101 Shaky rebirth

Quite typical of the post-war situation is this picture—military engineers resting for a while, as a train pulls gingerly across an improvised bridge 'somewhere in Germany'. Restoration of the lines and engineering works was one of the biggest problems faced in the immediate post-war years but note also the motley collection of stock and the standard Reichsbahn 'war locomotive' working tender first; depot and turning facilities were obvious targets for Allied fighters.

REHABILITATION

102 UNRRA 2-8-0

One of the vital needs after 1945 was to get communications working again in the war-shattered countries of Europe and the Far East. To help in this work, large batches of locomotives were built for the relief organisations, notable among which was the United Nations Rehabilitation and Relief Association (UNRRA). UNRRA locomotives of very similar design could be seen all over the place, and a typical type was this 2-8-0 produced by, among others, Vulcan Locomotive Works in Lancashire. Known as the 'Liberation' class it was a heavy freight locomotive with sustained tractive effort of no less than 46,380lb and a weight in working order of no less than $142\frac{1}{2}$ tons. Somewhat surprisingly in view of the rickety state of many railways, the maximum permitted axle-load was no less than 18·5 tons and the locomotive was provided only with the Westinghouse air brake.

103 141R (S.N.C.F.)

Other locomotives, while not provided specifically as part of the rehabilitation process, also owed their existence entirely to the war. Notable among these were the very successful series of 2-8-2 mixed-traffic machines, built by the Americans for France after the war. These, the S.N.C.F.'s 141R class, were built to a French specification but came out American in almost every detail. They were extremely competent locomotives, becoming maids-of-all-work on every region of the S.N.C.F. and were the final S.N.C.F. steam locomotives in regular use. Leading dimensions were: length overall 14·64m; coupled wheel diameter 1·62m; weight in working order 115·5t.

BRINGING THEM BACK

Just as after World War 1, the end of World War 2 found the Allied armed forces with a vast array of railway material, most of which was surplus to their peace-time requirements. At the same time there were a great many civilian railways, especially in occupied Europe, that were desperately short of motive power. The result was inevitable. The military locomotives had been specially designed to be as adaptable as possible—they had light axle-loads, a restricted loading gauge and were simple rugged machines since no one knew where they might have to run. They were, therefore, usable by almost any railway on which they happened to end up and the hard pressed railways took full advantage of the situation. Together with large quantities of enemy machines brusquely requisitioned as 'reparations', Allied army were shipped hither and thither, and locomotives of all types became common sights across Europe and the Middle East. Considering they were designed for a short hard life they lasted surprisingly well; a number were still doing useful work well into the 1970s.

PAINT IT WHAT COLOUR YOU LIKE

Not least among all these were the humble shunting tank locomotives that had been produced in quantity for use in the marshalling yards. In the British Isles, most popular was undoubtedly the standard Austerity 0-6-0ST (Pl. 48), only a comparative few of which saw civilian service abroad. Quite the opposite situation occurred with its American equivalent, a chunky 0-6-0 side tank which the U.S. Army Transportation Corps brought over to Europe in considerable numbers.

105 The basic locomotive

The locomotive in military guise was a typically 'American' side-tank design with two sandboxes atop the boiler, a full cab with back bunker and a smokebox of smaller diameter than the boiler cladding and secured (Baldwin fashion) by 'dogs' round the edge. The tanks were of conventional switcher pattern, sloping towards the front, and no running-boards were provided. Makers were H. K. Porter, Vulcan and Davenport. Leading dimensions were: length overall 29ft 6½in.; coupled wheelbase 10ft; wheel diameter 4ft 6in.; cylinders 16in. × 20in. Weight in working order was 47·05 tonnes and the steam brake was fitted.

106 S.N.C.F. version

Even after the war a few remained in military service, as with this example at Longmoor.

107 British Railways

Even British Railways 'came into' a few examples, as heirs to the Southern Railway, the latter having bought some in for shunting around its railway works in particular. Again, these survived many British designs, several lasting until phased out by dieselisation. Indeed, somewhat ironically, while many well-established British tank locomotives have not been preserved, at least two U.S.A. Tanks have been bought by privately-owned tourist railways in this country.

108 Yankee in Yorkshire

This shows one, on the Keighley and Worth Valley Railway, north-west of Leeds. Its new owners have painted it in their idea of typical American livery, an odd gesture for a class which never bore such colours. None the less it undeniably looks handsome with its rich brown tanks, black cab and aluminium-coloured smokebox, and is well liked.

TODAY

World War 2 established without any doubt that in a major conflict railways could only be used as an effective means of communication by the side retaining air superiority; with their fixed routes, dependence on vulnerable heavy engineering works such as bridges, and difficulty of camouflage they were too easy to knock out on a large scale. Furthermore the use of single prime movers for large tonnages of cargo made them even more vulnerable to air strikes. Attack a road convoy and some at least of the individual vehicles are likely to get through; disable the locomotive of a train and the whole thing is at your mercy. In any war where 'enemy' territory is being occupied the railways, for the same reasons, proved very vulnerable to sabotage as has been shown in most of the smaller campaigns since 1945. Lastly, modern wars are wars of movement and a more flexible form of supply is required except in safely established rear areas; it is symptomatic that all the major powers have been steadily 'running down' the railways sections of their transport organisations. The main British Army base at Longmoor, for instance, has now lost its training railway entirely and the permanent stock of motive power and equipment has been greatly reduced. Current experiments are concerned more with improvised use of existing rail tracks where required, as shown in Pls. 109 and 110.

POST-WAR ROAD/RAIL CONVERSIONS

109 Land Rover road/railer

Since the war various experiments have been made by the R.E. and later the Royal Corps of Transport with the ubiquitous Land Rover converted to rail use. In general these have been made with MT vehicles loaned to the old railway shops at Longmoor and returned to MT stock after the experiments were completed. Perhaps the most elaborate was this short-wheel base pick-up modified as a 'road/rail' vehicle. It retained its normal road tyres but had hydraulically operated guide-trucks fore and aft. These were kept in the raised position for road work but they could be lowered to act as guide wheels once the vehicle had been driven on to railway track.; conveniently the wheels of the ordinary road vehicle are spaced correctly for use on standard-gauge rails. The concept is not new and has never been very successful; there is no evidence that this was an exception.

110 Land Rover: semi-permanent conversion

Rather simpler were the experiments in the 1960s with a standard Mk 8 Land Rover pick-up. In these the normal road wheels were replaced by bolted on rail-wheels, using the existing axles and trials were carried out to find out what loads the vehicle could pull. The trials appear to have been generally successful —as with the wartime Jeep the Land

Rover has four-wheel drive and a wide selection of gears—but the conversions were not permanent. The experimental vehicles were returned to MT use after the trials were finished though it is reasonable to assume that conversion kits exist. Both standard- and metre-gauge versions were tried out, the plate showing the latter which required some modification owing to the reduced wheel-track.

THE MODERN PROBLEMS

111 Ambush drill

Typical of the modern approach to use of troops on railways is the accepted need to respond at short notice to 'enemy' attacks on a train. A complete drill has been worked out in various countries for providing the appropriate action in any emergency. These British troops, armed with the FN automatic rifle, are using a brake-van as a convenient 'stand' for practising riot drill—as might be deduced from the fact that they are not taking cover. Similar drills are available to allow train guards to react quickly and effectively against 'incidents' *en route* through disturbed country.

112 Full circle

This plate shows the reason why: the first picture in *Railways and War before 1918* showed the first guerrillas wrecking the first effective military rail communications, in the American Civil War. This last view shows that with modern explosives and other devices, it is very easy for small groups of determined men to wreck the installations of a railway so frequently as to make it unusable. An attacker or even a defender in 'unsympathetic' country as in Vietnam cannot effectively patrol huge lengths of railway and the actions of guerrillas are almost impossible to prevent. The campaigns in South-East Asia have shown that, even with air superiority, it is the attitude of people in any given area that will determine whether its railways are viable. Railways are still the most efficient carriers of supplies in bulk but they can only operate for military purposes in a pacified region.

113 It'll never replace the train

This tailpiece may appear flippant, but it does sum up succinctly the history of railways in war. They started by being regarded very dubiously; were only seized upon by the military after their efficiency as carriers had been very thoroughly proved (it'll never replace the horse!); and became indispensable adjuncts to any army's lines of supply only when the seeds of their downfall were already apparent. Attempts to use them offensively, with armoured trains, were foiled by the inherent disadvantage of any railway: in its fixed and vulnerable tracks. In effect the static conditions of World War 1 probably gave a spurious sense of importance to railway transport for its problems again became obvious as soon as aircraft and guerrillas —modern equivalents of the old Boer commandos—were able to interfere. It was these, and the increasing motorisation of armies, that led to the decline in military railway use after World War 2. Yet the problems of supply are still there; it takes a hundred ten-ton lorries or the equivalent capacity in aircraft to carry the load of one train. One wonders what *will* replace the railway if another major conventional conflict comes.

INDEX TO ILLUSTRATIONS

Africa, 2, 60, 61
Air attacks, 58, 59, 70
Ambush, 96, 112
Ardovia viaduct, 9
Armoured locomotives, 51
Armoured trains, 23, 24, 30, 31, 32, 63–4, 65, 66, 98
Armoured vehicles on rails, 67, 68, 99, 100
Artillery on rails, 33
Austria, 7–14

Bielefeld viaduct, 69
Buses on rails, 75, 76, 77

Camouflage, 58, 59
Colonial railways, 25, 52, 53
Convertible vehicles, 11, 12, 75, 76, 77, 92–3, 99–100, 109, 110

Destruction of railways, 17, 69, 94–5, 96, 112
Diesels, 54, 55, 56, 62

Egypt, 2
Evacuation, 29

Far East, 99–100
Farewells, 28, 29
Field railways, 25, 73

Garratts, 52, 53
Gas-producers, 75–6
Generator train, 11

Italy, 7–14, 62

Japanese railways, 99, 100

Kriegslokomotives, 34, 35, 36

Light railways,
  British, 26, 32, 74
  Continental, 14, 15, 19, 20, 70, 72, 73
Loads, 82, 83, 84
Locomotives,
  American, 41, 42, 56, 57, 87, 105, 109
  Austrian, 7, 10
  Belgian, 19
  British, 26, 30, 46, 47, 54, 57, 74
  French, 103
  German, 21, 22, 34–40, 55, 73
  Russian, 43, 44, 45

Mallet locomotives, 25
Maps, 3, 14

Narrow-gauge, 1–6, 10, 13, 14, 19, 20, 25, 26, 32, 61, 72, 73, 74, 108

Palestine, 1

Railway loads, 79, 80–84
Rehabilitation, 101, 102, 103
Rolling-stock, 25, 26, 27, 34, 35, 61, 62, 81, 82
Romney Hythe & Dymchurch LR, 32
Russian front, 30–8, 42–5, 63, 64, 94–5

Salonika, 3–6
Ships, 85–91
Shropshire & Montgomeryshire LR, 26, 74
SNCV, 19, 80

Tanks, 67, 68, 84, 97, 99

Verdun, battle of, 15–18